Whose Apple Is It Anyway!

Empowering Purpose to Achieve Your God-Ordained Destiny
Second Edition

Linda F. Williams, MSW

Whose Apple Press
Grand Rapids, Michigan

Copyright © 2017 Linda F. Williams.

All rights reserved. No portion of this book may be reproduced, stored in a retrieval system, or transmitted in any form or by any means — electronic, mechanical, photocopy, recording, scanning, or other — except for brief quotations in critical reviews or articles, or as specifically allowed by the U. S. Copyright Act of 1976, as amended, without the prior written permission of the publisher.

Published by Whose Apple Press LLC, Grand Rapids, Michigan

Unless otherwise noted, Scripture quotations are from the King James Version.

Scripture quotations designated NKJV are from the New King James Version, copyright 1979, 1980, 1982, Thomas Nelson, Inc., Publishers.

Scripture taken from The Message. Copyright © 1993, 1994, 1995, 1996, 2000, 2001, 2002.
Used by permission of NavPress Publishing Group.

Library of Congress Control Number: 2017902391

ISBN-13: 978-0-692-84604-9
ISBN-10: 0-692-84604-2

Cover Design: DH Bonner Virtual Solutions
Cover Art: Copyright © Linda F. Williams. All Rights Reserved.

Interior Design: Richard Toland and Linda F. Williams
Printed in the United States of America

Dedication

*To my precious parents,
the late Junius "Bill" Williams, who held my destiny in his heart until his
last breath, refusing to let it go; and Frances Williams, who through
prayer, encouragement, affirmation, and firm spiritual guidance, acted
as my spiritual midwife as this dream was brought forth.*

*To Little Sister, Susan A. Williams, for the spiritual conversation that
sparked a forgotten memory of the book you now hold in your hands.*

*To Baby Sister, the late Judith S. Williams, for inspiring the first
chapter and spearheading the dream.*

*Dedicated to the memory of Whitney Elizabeth Houston and Debra
Foran, who each, through triumph and tragedy, remained steadfast in
their love for God.*

The path of purpose is paved with healing. Healing goes as deep as the wound or as deep as you let it.

- Linda F. Williams

Contents

Dedication V

Contents IX

Preface XI

Acknowledgements XV

Introduction XVII

Chapter 1: The Root of the Matter 32

Chapter 2: The Fruit of the Matter 79

Chapter 3: Whose Apple is it, Anyway! 87

Chapter 4: Hone Your Harvest 115

Chapter 5: Date with Destiny 139

Plain Talk: Terminology 153

About the Author 169

Preface

You would not believe the spiritual and emotional turmoil I went through finishing this book! Relationships went to heck in a hand basket. I didn't know which way was up. At one point, it was a constant struggle with old issues as I scuffled to wrestle that old Linda back into her cage.

This book emerged as I lived and learned the truths I'm about to share. These lessons were not neatly acquired through academics. They are the result of decades at the University of Hard Knocks. As I conclude this seven-year voyage, it's evident that absent those lessons this book would remain, in perpetuity, a work in progress.

Mistakes and all, this is my life on these pages. My specific instructions were to be compassionate toward my enemies and wrongdoers and be honest about myself. That's backwards compared to how we usually live. We usually judge others harsher than ourselves; it's easier to focus on the perceived weaknesses of others than it is to address our own. But, I had to quit running, turn around, and face myself before I could confront hidden, deep-seated issues. It's funny. I was hoofing it trying to get away from something, the whole time clueless as to what it was chasing me down. It's been a healing journey.

Concept

This book's concept emerged during a discussion about relationships, the lack of personal responsibility, and the human propensity toward the blame game. I thought of Adam and Eve, who each blamed someone or something else for their individual decisions to "do the goofy" by disobeying God.

Adam blamed both God and Eve, and Eve pointed at the serpent. Each blamed someone or something else for the choices they made, and nobody was claiming that apple. Not even the joker who started the whole mess! Where was the serpent while Eve was blaming him? The truth is it wasn't about the apple or the ensuing blame game. What's really at the core of that fiasco went unnoticed.

I had come up with a book title and concept, but as life's drama unfolded, I forgot about the discussion and the book. Over a decade later, on December 17, 2005, I received a fateful phone call from my sister, Susan. She said I was going to write a book. That otherwise outlandish statement struck a chord, confirming one of my mother's earlier predictions. Thinking back, I remembered I had come up with a title for a book, but I couldn't, for the life of me, remember what it was. I hung up, walked into the kitchen, and in one fell swoop asked God for both clarity and confirmation, saying, "Lord, if You want me to write this book, You're going to have to give me that title again." Bam! I had barely finished the sentence before in it rushed, and for the next five years, *It Ain't All About Eve, and It Ain't Adam's Apple* became the title.

I would write off and on over the years, knowing I had more living and learning to do before the book could be finished. Who knew when the final ink would dry? Many asked. I had no answers. About five years passed before I finally hired a writing coach, Nancy Peske, coauthor of *Raising a Sensory Smart Child: The Definitive Handbook for Helping Your Child with Sensory Processing Issues*.[1] She made many informed suggestions, all of which were a challenge. On her advice, I struggled to shorten the title, researching what I had come up with. This story nailed it! This is my paraphrase:

> *One day an old man was relaxing peacefully beneath a tree when an irate man walked up and started chewing him out for being a beggar. I mean the man called him everything under the sun until he realized he was receiving no reaction.*
>
> *Finally, frustrated with getting no response, he fumed, "How can you sit there so calmly while I'm yelling at you? Didn't you hear what I said?"*

Reaching into his begging basket, the old man pulled out an apple. Holding it out to the angry man, he answered with this question: "If I have an apple, and I give it to you, but you don't take it, whose apple is it?"

The angry man answered, "Well it's yours of course," to which the old man replied, "You offer me insults and anger, and I choose not to take it, so the insults and anger are yours, not mine."

The story was about Buddha, but it's a slam-dunk description of the concept for this book. It demonstrates how only *we* control our own inner emotions, as opposed to others controlling them. We can choose to internalize negative experiences, or we can leverage them. The choice between the two determines whether we remain victims of, or victors over, our pasts! We choose our reactions to situations or circumstances. Our responses empower or destroy our futures. If not aligned with purpose, calling, and mission, our behaviors can short-circuit our destiny.

Footage Firm © 2014 All Right Reserved. Used by Permission.

Empowerment: Break the Chains of the Past

This is about freedom, my friend! It's your personal road map to freedom from the insidious fear and bondage that blocks purpose. It's about empowering life choices in spite, sometimes in the middle, of bad experiences. It's about courage to step out from behind a façade of counterproductive defenses to conquer one by one the spiritual roadblocks that short-circuit God's plan for you. It's about empowerment and leveraging the change it takes to realize your purpose and fulfill your God- ordained destiny.

Game Changer

Empowerment begins with leveraging choice. This life-changing truth is the answer to any challenge in any area of your emotional or spiritual life.

This is a game changer, my friend. It positions you for peak performance in your career. It facilitates sound professional and personal relationships. It recalibrates your thinking and puts you back on track to destiny.

Take a quick inventory. Is there someplace you're stuck? Are you going another round with the same old thing? What about your career? Is it a job or a joy? Do you ever get the feeling you might have missed your calling? What would you rather be doing with your life? By the way, remember that childhood dream you had to either do or be something when you grew up? Whatever happened to that? You'll discover the answers to these questions and more as you leverage what's revealed in these pages. You're about to take a powerful journey. So take a deep breath and exhale a hardy good-bye to the current status quo!

No matter how your life has been up to now. No matter what challenges you face, it's a new day, and you're about to leverage the power to change it all. That's right! Right now, right where you stand, you can take control of it all by simply *changing your mind*.

Acknowledgements

Nancy Peske, coach extraordinaire. Without you, I'd still be feeling in the dark.

Bill Carmichael, thanks for knowing when to send an email to kick me in the pants.

Fredrick "Stay Tuned" Longmire, for numerous spiritual conversations over hair glue and hairdryers. Your sweet and loving spirit is eclipsed only by your love for God.

Introduction

Let me ask you something. No masks, no facades, no pretense. It's going to take a deliberate minute to focus past all that, so take your time. There's nobody here but us. Be honest. I'm talking about taking it straight to places few, if any, have ever been as you answer these questions to yourself:

- Are you baffled by multiple trips to the altar about the same old thing that inevitably comes back to haunt you?
- Are you in a recurring or relentless cycle of guilt after multiple trips through the prayer line that ended with the disappointment of realizing it didn't auto-magically change you or your life?
- Have you ever accused yourself of having too little faith because nothing you've tried has worked the way you thought it would?
- When it doesn't work, are you left wondering where you've gone wrong?
  Have you ever gone through the unyielding grip of shame, fear, victimization, and/or addictions?
- Are you reluctant to talk about these challenges with others? Are you putting on your "church face" to cover up?
- Are you enjoying considerable success in your career or ministry, yet you're unable to shake the nagging feeling that something is missing or just not quite right?
- Do you see any life patterns that might be holding you back? Do you wind up in the same relationship drama again and again?

A yes answer to any of these questions means you are one of many of us facing similar spiritual challenges. Maybe that's where we went wrong.

We've been majoring in the spiritual at the expense of the one thing we all share — our humanity. No wonder we're stuck. We've been duped into turning our backs on the realities of human existence, as if any consideration of it is sinful.

We're told the flesh is to be subdued at all cost. Don't give in to it. Ignore it. Deny it. If it rears its ugly head, start praying. There's no room from that perspective for understanding our humanity, and in that, my friend, lies the missing link that stands between you and the inside-out healing only found along the Path of Purpose.

Because we think we're the odd man out, we put on our well-developed Christian masks and privately wonder at those around us who seem to have it all together. We follow their lead — praying in tongues, binding the devil, jumping up and down, and praising the Lord — all in the name of spiritual warfare. Yet when the emotional dust settles, we're still saddled with recurring negative relationships, unrelenting habits, addictions, anger, fear, and you name it. In these areas, we still suffer defeat because we can holler and scream at the devil until the cows come home. It has no effect on our minds, and it does little to affect the inside-out healing it takes to overcome a painful past.

It's like yelling, "Giddy up!" wondering why we're not going anywhere. We can't even claim the cart-before-horse issue as an excuse because the horse is back at the ranch. You need the cart *and* the horse to make progress. One without the other won't do. As long as we are human, we can't ignore the humanity-spirituality dynamic. I'm not saying miraculous things haven't happened. If God wants to miraculously remove decades of pain, He's the one to do it. By considerable measure, though, few of us have that experience. When we don't, we're faced with self-accusations of too little faith.

As a church, we've done ourselves a disservice by ignoring the realities of the human condition and its relationship to the soul connection. We can't turn our backs on our humanity and expect victory. We can't ignore years of sound behavioral science. It takes a balance of the two to devise a fail-proof war strategy that *flips the script* on enemy mind games.

What You'll Find

Described as *The Battlefield of the Mind*[1] meets *The Purpose Driven Life*[2] against a backdrop of the Master Plan, here you'll learn why what we've been taught about our flesh is off focus, why the soul is the prime target, and why the mind is the battlefield. You'll learn to wield the one weapon you've had all along and gain the skill to leverage it to navigate enemy *mind*-fields devised to redirect focus and sidetrack purpose.

You're about to:

- Discover the subtle secret Eve overlooked in the Garden of Eden and how the enemy has used the same old strategy to steal focus and usurp vision. You'll gain the tools to recognize, root out, and leverage it toward achieving your vision.
- Learn to avoid the perpetual mistake Adam and Eve made after eating the forbidden fruit.
- See what is at the core of why Israel was turned back at their Border of Destiny. Discover what they carried out of Egypt that held them captive to a total eclipse of the mind that landed them within arm's reach of a dream they could not see. You'll gain the insight to avoid this destiny-destroying pitfall.
- Learn how to leverage adversity and redirect purpose by increasing your *Apple*tude (emotional aptitude), leveraging the APPLE Inventory, and activating the FRUITS Philosophy for destiny-driven results that are based in mission and purpose.

Here you'll find keys that unlock the chains of the past by exposing blind spots that become major points of enemy attack. You'll achieve and maintain once-and-for-all freedom from the inside out. By identifying what seeds lie at the core of issues, you'll gain the skill to quickly cut to the root of any situation or circumstance and emerge victorious, no matter what the challenge.

What You Won't Find

This is not your grandmother's self-help book. This is real talk for real people in a real world. You won't find typical religious terminology that leaves you confused as to what to do next or what it means in *your* life. Concepts are discussed with new millennium relevance that won't leave you pie-in-the- sky perplexed. This is plain talk, pure and simple. Phrases such as "Have the mind of Christ," "Know who you are in Christ" and "In the flesh" give way to real-world relevance. So let's dig in and lay the groundwork for things to follow by demystifying some of the confusion.

Before We Begin

Before you begin chapter one, it is important that you read the "Plain Talk: Terminology" section at the back of the book. This is foundational to all the concepts in this book, and without an understanding of them, you will likely not be able to keep up with the discussion.

In the interest of housekeeping, you'll note that throughout the text I use phrases such as *"What if..."* or *"I choose to believe..."* These phrases are deliberately employed in places where there is either ongoing theological debate, or I am discussing views that might not be specifically stated in Scripture. Okay. Let's de-mystify some often-misunderstood terms.

Groundwork

The truth is our foundation and the Bible, as the Word of Truth, is our compass (see Psalm 119:160 and Daniel 10:21). Jesus, as "the way, truth, and life" (John 14:6) sets our example. God is the originator of truth. Truth is absolute. It transcends culture and human inclination.[1] These truths are unchanging. I call them Cultivating Principles.

Cultivating Principles

Accept it or not, there are eternal, immutable laws governing the universe, including you. Whether you call them universal or spiritual laws, they apply to everybody and everything. These truths set the parameters for change. We can't move forward as long as we deny their existence. How we align ourselves with these principles determines our ultimate outcomes.

It doesn't matter whether we understand why, agree, or disagree. These principles are established truth. Nobody gets a free pass from them. So, whether you are part of the fake-it-'til-you-make-it crowd or the believe- it-and-achieve-it crowd, leveraging these truths, these Cultivating Principles, positions you for success. They are the ground in which your roots should be anchored.

Can't Fake the Fruit — Sowing and Reaping

The principle of sowing and reaping was among the very first foundational truths Jesus taught the disciples. Some have referred to it as the Law of Attraction, which aptly describes how it works. The law of reaping and sowing demonstrates a universal law that is easier described than applied. How you consistently respond to less than stellar situations and circumstances is what sets up your own future harvest or outcomes. *"You get as good as you give"* and whatever seed you plant in life will determine the crop you get back. Jesus considered this a no-brainer, yet the disciples didn't understand it. When they asked Him what it meant (Mark 4:13), He more or less answered, *"Dude! If you don't get this, I may as well pack it in. Everything I'm here to teach you depends on it. You've got to get this, you guys!"*

That's rather plain language, if you ask me. We can't fake the fruit, folks. Fool ourselves as we may; whatever we sow (plant) we reap (get back). This can be either the boomerang dynamic or the boomerang debacle, because the final outcome swings on what kind of seed (behaviors or reactions) you are tossing about. You get as good as you give, and whatever you think becomes your reality (see Proverbs 23:6–8). It is what it is, and that's all it is.

Supporting how serious God is about this, Paul later warned in Galatians 6:8 not to fool ourselves. God's not playing around. Whatever fruit we're tossing will surely result in a commensurate crop. We plant our future harvests by our own choices and reactions to life. Every word from our mouths, every act, good or bad, plants a seed that surely produces a future harvest, and it all begins with a thought. Count on it!

What Were You Thinking? Creative Thought

What we think creates our realties because thoughts drive how we act. (See Proverbs 23:7.) Thoughts are fueled by what is lingering in our souls (in our hearts). That said, we are in a lot of trouble when our thought life is undisciplined. When we have years of trauma crowding out vision, we are not capable of destiny-driven decisions because our minds are God's natural enemies. Water seeks its own level, and your life will sink or swim depending on how you think about it. Drop a straw into it a glass of water, cover the top of the straw with your finger, and then pull it partially out of the glass. Now let go, and the water level in the straw returns to the water level in the glass.

Look around and think about where you are in your life right now. Then think back a few months, a year, or even a few years. What were you thinking? How were you thinking? What choices did you make that led to your current situation, and is this a repeating pattern in your life? If something doesn't change, count on more of the same, because it is going to *take* that change to seed a better future. The higher our thoughts (water in the glass), the clearer the vision, and the more destiny-driven decisions we are able to make. Our lives will reach the highest or the lowest level of our thoughts. Thoughts (even subconscious ones) are self-fulfilling prophecies because they drive our behaviors and seed our future harvests.

Why Are You Here? Creative Purpose

Because He is a God of order, God creates nothing without a conceived purpose. We can call this His Creative Purpose. If you're breathing and have a belly button, you have a purpose. Thank heaven for that! Imagine the cosmic mess we would be in if God created things without purpose or reason. Willy-nilly throwing out whatever comes to mind just because He can. No, He is a God of ordered purpose where all things work in harmony, in His divine order. As Jeremiah 29:11 says, he has a reason for each of us.

God's predetermined Creative Purpose for you is not some riddle floating around the cosmos waiting to be figured out. It's clearly stated in His Word, and you need only recognize your own natural bent to find your specific purpose. We are fully equipped for our callings and predestined by His Creative Purpose to fulfill them. The fact that you are here is testament to your purpose in His Master Plan. Your personality, talent, and abilities are no accident. You are uniquely equipped for executing your role in the Master Plan.

Cosmic Chess Game — Predestination and Free Will

Any debate over free will versus predestination would end if opposing parties agreed that they are not mutually exclusive; they work in tandem. God could have created Adam and Eve without freedom of choice. He chose not to. He predestined them to a life of ease in direct relationship with Him. They *chose* to obey a different voice, summarily handing over earthly dominion to Satan. In this case, the Garden of Eden is God's Creative Purpose. He created Adam and Eve out of the ground on which they walked. Everything in them screamed purpose, and they lived the destiny He created for them. Yet Adam and Eve ate the forbidden fruit, short-circuiting the Master Plan and with it the purpose for which they had been created. Seeing the end from the beginning, God redeemed the whole mess through Jesus. But the root of this perpetuates to this very day. Because of free will we choose to cooperate or not. It's an easier road to go for all involved when we cooperate. It's like a cosmic chess game.

Cosmic Chess Game

Imagine life as a chess game. The opponents are God and Satan. We are God's army, His chess pieces. Satan's army is anybody who falls for his manipulation. God is trying to maneuver us through enemy territory to the Border of Destiny. Any chance of conquering God's side of the chessboard went out the window for Satan eons ago when he decided he was some kind of match for God. So his focus is mucking up God's game plan.

It's the only battle strategy he has left. His plan is weakened by the fact that it only works with our cooperation. Who wins each battle is pretty much up to us.

The Objective

In chess, the objective is to corner the king so he has nowhere to go — checkmate! Each opponent devises playing strategies with that end in mind. The move at hand is never the primary focus. Strategizing multiple moves in advance, each opponent anticipates the other's reaction to a specific movement on the board. Consequently, each strategy builds on the other until the objective is accomplished. It's a major mind game in which each opponent tries to out-think the other.

PhotoDune © 2014. All Right Reserved. Used by Permission.

In the cosmic version of this game, there is no intellectual contest between Satan and God, because God sees the end from the beginning, and nothing can take Him by surprise. Satan, however, knowing he's no match for God, employs distraction and innuendo in an effort to attack God's intent and instruction. He can't influence God; he can only influence us, and only to the degree we allow it.

Game Rules

In chess each piece has its designated place in the beginning lineup, and each piece moves according to its designated movement capabilities. For example, a knight can move two steps in either direction and then one step to the right or left. In this cosmic version of the game, the pieces get to choose to go along with God's direction, or they can change the game by refusing to go along and doing something else. Can anybody say, "Free will?"

Opponent Strategies

Opponent A — Team Destiny: God, captain of Team Destiny, is Grandmaster and Creator of the game. He set the rules, He never breaks them. His play is deliberate and concise. He never reneges on a move. Once He sets His mind to something, it's a done deal. He is playing from an omnipresent perspective, meaning He sees beyond all dimensions of the playing field. He knows the outcome from the beginning of play. For Him excellence is the standard, victory the goal.

Opponent B — Team Destruction: As captain of Team Destruction, Satan's strategy is three-pronged: to steal, kill, and destroy (see John 10:10).

- **Steal:** Satan attempts to steal vision at every strategic opportunity. Just as when driving a car we tend to steer in the direction of our gaze, shifting focus away from purpose sends us off course. You can't drive in a direction opposite to your gaze. Misdirected focus equals stolen vision.
- **Kill:** Satan plans to kill every bit of hope for your future. This subtle ploy is progressive and can happen completely without notice. Until we rediscover hope, we don't even realize it's gone. It's like falling asleep at the wheel — you don't realize you are asleep until you are waking up.
- **Destroy:** Satan plans to destroy every destiny-related aspect of your personality, character, and talents. Why? They are our divine equipment — the part of our tool kit

that renders them powerful or powerless. From a spiritual standpoint, as it relates or our destinies, our tool kits are our divine birthright because they are part and parcel to our whole reason for existence.

Our personalities are intrinsically germane to actualizing the purpose necessary to realize our God-determined destinies. By distorting this core aspect of our beings, Satan effectively cripples the spiritual and personal growth necessary to recognize, realize, and appreciate our callings. Failure to recognize this ploy blocks inside-out healing that is only found along our own purposeful paths. You will never reach your destiny if you are off your Path of Purpose. Now that we've introduced the opponents and have an overview of their chosen strategies, we join the game in progress.

Let the Games Begin

Let's say midway in the game God moves you, a rook. You can only see a square- length in any direction. A quick glance around and you don't see any knight of your color, so you decide you are a knight and act accordingly. You jump one square off, taking out one of Satan's men in the offing. Aren't you the wise one? Let's ask the officials.

You're judged as making an illegal move because rooks can't jump other pieces. Meanwhile, back at the ranch, the dude you took out is back in battle, and you are sidelined! The problem is you are still a rook, regardless of your so-called disguise. It fools nobody, as evidenced by the fact that you are sidelined along with your queen, leaving your king vulnerable to attack at the next move. Congratulations, you just gave up ground to the opponent and jeopardized others to boot. You got off your square, now Satan has it, and Team Destiny has to navigate a last-minute change in the game plan.

In the end, and from the beginning, God wins. That fight was fixed before time itself. But each decision we make (subconsciously or deliberately) is a choice for or against that plan. Choose calling, mission, and purpose, and you get your God- designed destiny. Choose otherwise, you don't. Simple. We don't come here with every decision preprogrammed and our life experiences lined up as in a sitcom script. Because our own choices create our personal outcomes, we can change the game at will.

It is not predestination (insert creepy music here) as if God orchestrated the wrong we have endured. We can't blame God for others' decisions and deeds. We can't blame Him for our own choices and behaviors and we surely can't blame Him for our results.

How you play the game is up to you. Every time your choices don't align with purpose, mission, and destiny, it causes a delay of game and holds up resources God intended to channel to others through you.

If life is tough right now, know that even in the middle of the most chaotic mess, God did His part before you got there. It is not too late to create a better result. Destiny is on your side. What side of destiny are you on? Now that we've laid the groundwork, let's move forward to find out just what bogus fruit might be lurking in our harvest. We begin in the middle of the mess that spearheaded this project.

Chapter 1: The Root of the Matter

How did I get into this mess? Broken down, broke, torn down, and fed up. Until now I've barely survived robbing Peter to pay Paul. Now Peter's crying broke! I was tired of an empty tank, empty refrigerator, and empty soul. I was being garnished so much I had nothing left to pay rent.

Meanwhile the voice of my landlord l o o p e d incessantly. Like the soundtrack of an old movie where the character is losing her mind. It reverberated loudly as it slowly faded to an echoed drone, "I'd hate to have to forcibly remove you from the premises."

Divorce debt was breaking my financial back, and being hit with a $712 per month garnishment broke the bank. About a month before it all hit the fan I had catalogued all my bills, spreadsheet and all. Before it was over, I was glad I did. At the time, I had no way of knowing that the next couple of weeks would land me in the office of a bankruptcy lawyer. Twenty minutes into the appointment, even he was overwhelmed, saying, *"I've been in family law for ten years, but I have never seen anything like this."*

Suggesting a second opinion, he referred me to a colleague with expertise in restructuring student loans. I should have recognized it as the blow-off it was, because that so-called expert never called me back. When I came back to the guy, he summarily refused the case. By then I was beyond irritated. But okay. Maybe that was God's way of telling me that was not the route to take.

I went back home, tail between my legs, to regroup. I then came across a Christian debt-counseling site. Yeah, that's the ticket, I thought. I'll get an opinion from a Christian organization. I filled out the forms figuring, by the next day, I might get a response.

Ten-thirty that evening the phone rang. What are they doing calling me so late at night? Two minutes into it I heard, *"Get to a lawyer now!"*

After hearing that statement three times in the same conversation, I must have looked shocked. I knew the principles of the organization, so I knew things were rather serious because the last thing I expected to hear was, *"Get to a lawyer now!"*

I tried once more to reach the recommended expert bankruptcy lawyer. On the phone, his assistant said that he had agreed to take my case for a thousand dollars, but where was I going to get a thousand dollars? It was as if I was on fire, and the fireman was asking *me* for a hose. If I'd had that kind of money, l wouldn't have been sitting there. I just didn't have it. I couldn't ignore the hint of hopelessness in the assistant's voice, asking, "What do you have?"

"I have the two hundred fifty dollars I was going to give the other guy." The music that played as she put me on hold did little to allay my anxiety as I awaited my fate.

"Okay, she said, "he said he will take the case since you were referred by his colleague." Great. Maybe there is an end to this financial hell on earth. I made the appointment and got in the same day. Placing my perfectly organized binder before the assistant, I explained I had until Monday to answer an eviction notice.

"*I think you had better plan on moving,*" the lawyer warned upon joining the meeting. "*The best we can do is to buy some time — maybe about a month.*"

He decided to contact the landlord to see about payment arrangements, and that sounded good to me. I had nothing to lose for the effort. At least the lawyer would get the garnishment off my back, and it felt good to unload that three-pound binder I'd been lugging around as an appendage.

When I got home, I turned on the television, and mindlessly stared at the screen. I wasn't eating, barely sleeping, and another mental breakdown was nipping at my heels like a blood-crazed pitbull. One false move and I would be in its merciless grip. I did everything I could not to think or feel. I couldn't chance "losing it" again.

One weekend I wound up at work knowing the office was closed. The next thing I knew, I was pacing the floor and crying out to God in hopeless desperation. I don't remember all I said, but I do remember telling Him, "*I am so frustrated! What is going on?*" You know the drill—the typical crybaby jag He has heard from all of us.

"*I am so angry! I don't know what's going on,*" I yelled. Little did I know that I was blaming everyone and everything for my own situation. Every relationship I had with a man ended in emotional and financial devastation. I was caught in a cycle of constant bad choices. There I was on the heels of my second divorce, and already I was caught in another relationship with a man that was nothing like what I desired or deserved. None of them ever were. I was a discombobulated, twisted, jumbled, hot mess consumed with anxiety, depression, anger, fear, confusion, and the loneliness of having to once again suck it up, stuff it, and deal with the drama that was my life. Bankruptcy and eviction were imminent.

I called my baby sister. I must have sounded pretty bad because all she said was, "*I'm on my way.*"

In a futile attempt to soothe myself, I started walking the office parking lot. I must have resembled a mad woman looking for a fight. Knowing from experience how aggressive the local geese were, I walked right through them, picturing myself on the corner of one of the busiest intersections in Grand Rapids, East Beltline and Leonard, windmill-swinging all comers as if each represented some idiot who had made my life miserable. Right then I could have taken them down one at a time!

Any other time they would be looking for a fight. At the slightest provocation, they would strike anybody leaving the building. But that day, just my luck, no takers.

I wondered aloud how I must have looked in that empty parking lot getting my march on, "*Maybe they'll think I'm out here exercising,*" One look at the cigarette I was madly puffing in marching band cadence, I thought, Dead giveaway — that can't be it. After a while, I just didn't care. I was going to walk until I fell out or felt better.

I looked up and saw my sister Judith's car (saved by the bell). We sat on the curb not saying much at first. With the desperation on my face, she probably didn't know whether to ask questions or make that call. I unloaded on her about my financial woes, relationship problems, and my entire miserable existence. I was tired of being let down all the time. Who was ever there for me when I needed it?

I had nothing to show for a miserable mess of a marriage other than a set of divorce papers and boatload of debt, all compliments of my ex-husband who, for the better part of the marriage, was either in prison or living the good life on my dime. I was tired of starting over alone. Breaking a lengthy silence, Judith called my attention to a little seagull meandering toward us. "*Look at him. He's not worried about anything,*" she laughed.

I looked at the little guy waddling around without a care or thought and said, "*Shoot, he doesn't have to make rent.*"

The youngest of three girls, Judith was the baby in the family. I'm the oldest, so I called her Baby Sister. Between us is Susan, Little Sister. But don't be fooled by birth order because, although she was the baby, we always said Judith was born thirty-years old. She just had a wiser soul. With a few well-placed words, she can deliver the truth with disarming impact, and the meaning is never in question. She'll make you laugh and cry as you recover from the blow, and in this case, she did not disappoint. I should have expected nothing less. She dropped the hammer. In eight simple words, she landed an indelibly resounding blow: "*You can't be in love with somebody's potential.*"

There it was. She knew me. She knew I saw others as God created them (their potential); the whole time ignoring what life experience had twisted them into. She was telling me it didn't matter how much good I saw in somebody. If they didn't see it, it may as well not exist, and no amount of my wishing otherwise was going to change it. My life was the result of ignoring that truth. One unhealthy, abusive, non-affirming relationship after another, I refused to see what life had twisted these men into. Sad commentary to admit the very thing I chose to ignore became my ultimate downfall.

My own perspective was so twisted by my own experiences I lost sight of the woman God created in me. That woman was nowhere to be found as I stumbled blindly, haphazardly, through one heartbreak after another, stuffing the trauma as I fooled myself into thinking I was over it. Instead of taking the time to process the emotional fallout, I just sucked it up and stepped it off. I never took time to acknowledge the pain, let alone work through it.

Before that last beat down (I won't mention how many others there were), I wore my heart on my sleeve, giving it, and myself, freely to anybody with a kind word, or whoever pretended to care about me. I got hurt so much I convinced myself I just didn't care anymore, which served no good purpose other than to perpetuate the problem. All my futile attempts at shielding myself did nothing to address the root of my problems.

Tough Girl

I went around for years with a chip on my shoulder everybody saw but me. I had endured so much. I was so caught up in denial I never saw any of it coming. Each blind-siding event dimmed my focus a little more.

Rather than embrace my sensitivity, I considered it a character flaw. I decided to protect myself at all cost, never realizing that the very essence of who I am was at stake. After years of one emotional defense mechanism, after the other, honest soul searching revealed that, in the interest of self- protection, I had completely disconnected from the things God instilled in me, everything I am at His creative hands. Everything I need to be to realize my purpose, mission, and destiny — all that represents my spiritual birthright, my tool kit. Without it, I could never reach my destiny.

I was affected by a long list of hurtful life experiences, from emotional breakdowns to rape to abortion to heartrending grief over being separated from my children. By the age of twenty-two, I had been a victim of domestic violence in my first marriage. After that I married a liar, drug addict, child molester, and rapist. No, that is not four different husbands. That's just my second husband.

I'll spare you the clown parade in between. Let's just say it didn't get any better because I kept right on fishing in the idiot barrel. The whole time I was indignant, hurt, and misunderstood after yet another disappointment, failed relationship, or trauma. I was stuck in some kind of God-forsaken holding pattern.

In response, I took on a tough-girl persona that kept everybody at bay. I just didn't care. But then I had the nerve to wonder why some people wanted nothing to do with me, why others related to me combatively, and why I kept drawing the wrong people into my life.

Meanwhile I was clueless at the helm as tough girl insidiously, gradually, progressively, and without my knowledge became entrenched. The more reality slapped me in the face, the deeper tough girl dug in. That persona took no prisoners where her survival was concerned, and it was no holds barred when it came to calling out the denial forces to back her up.

One day I was complaining to a couple of coworkers about yet another knucklehead I had met. Who knows, it might have been that time when I pulled a blade on some dude in a club for calling me an ugly name. Just because I didn't want to dance with him.

"*Why do I keep attracting guys like that?*" I asked. I wasn't ready for such a quick response: "*Because that's how you carry yourself.*"

Oh, boy. That felt like a truthful slap in the face. I knew there was something to it, but it would be decades before that truth caught up with me. It took years to figure out that the same compassion and sensitivity that got me into trouble were treasures, not liabilities. Once I did, I decided they should not be wasted on just anybody.

But to get there I needed to make better choices, and my whole outlook was so distorted it was mutating my true persona. Rather than accept that everybody walking the earth is not capable of comprehending, appreciating, embracing, or reciprocating my values, I just decided not to care. I turned my back on myself in the process, and there I was some thirty years later, separated from my second husband and on the verge of bankruptcy, homelessness, and another nervous breakdown.

It wasn't a stretch to decide to ask myself some serious questions: Why did I keep choosing wrong relationships? Do they feel "safer" to me? What was it that caused me to feel I didn't deserve any better?

Meanwhile, as I sat there that day with my baby sister, Joyce Meyer's words echoed through a canyon of emptiness: *"How long are you going to keep on going around that same old mountain?"* Only I wasn't one of the children of Israel; I was Moses — the guy who spent forty years on the back side of the desert *before* he spent forty years roaming through it again.

I had a decision to make if I was going to finally end the vicious cycle. Circumstances were screaming in my face that I had better do something differently. As my decision went, so would the rest of my life. Time was of the essences. I'd passed spring chicken stage a few barns back, and I wasn't even in sight of my Border of Destiny. Although Moses was denied admission to the Promised Land, at least he *did* get a *glimpse* of it. The way I was going, I wasn't even going to *see* mine.

Just Call Me Moses!

It occurred to me that I had Mosesitus. That means being so blind to our character flaws that even in the face of self-perpetuated consequences we don't see that *we* are the problem. We are still entrenched in the past without knowing it. We think it's the fault of unsuspecting others. We know enough to want better, but we can't make the connection to gain control. That was exactly where I was. Something in me knew there *was* better, *wanted* better, and decided to *wait* for better. In the end all the wanting, wishing, and waiting didn't do a thing to change my life.

Many years of self-isolation did result in some healing, but that process was halted by the fear of moving forward. When it came to taking that next step, I was fighting myself the whole way as if Destiny was in a struggle with my own stubborn will.

So, believe it or not, Moses — an old dude from the Bible — epitomized my life. His story illustrates the reason why overcoming this destiny destroyer is so personally, spiritually, and eternally important to fulfilling your purpose and realizing the destiny God has planned for you. So let's take a closer look at Moses and what his story means to our story.

Mosesitus: Desert-Forty Part I

To appreciate how remarkable Moses' story is and how it relates to our topic, let's take a step back in history and begin with how Israel wound up in Egypt in the first place. Then we will come back to Moses before we take a look at the core issues cloaking the hidden seed that kept Moses and most of the exiles out of the Promised Land.

Exile. You may remember the story in Genesis 30–50 of Joseph and his multicolored coat. Long before their father gave Joseph that magnificent garment, his brothers were jealous of Joseph's preferential treatment by their dad. He was his father's favorite. So when Joseph started bragging about recurring dreams, it didn't set well with the family that the dreams all ended with everybody bowing down to Joseph. Even his father chewed him out, asking if he really thought his parents would bow down to him. It was just too much.

One day Joseph's brothers plotted to kill him and make it look as though a wild animal had taken him out, coat and all. Thankfully, his older brother Ruben talked them out of that murderous plot. But they were determined to be rid of his braggy rump, one way or another, so they took his coat and threw him into a cistern, eventually selling him to a band of Ishmaelites on their way to Egypt. Long story short, God used their intended evil for good, and Joseph ultimately ruled Egypt as second-in-command. In that role, he saved all of Egypt by creating a plan to make the Egyptians the sole source of food during a devastating famine.

Pharaoh was so grateful he told Joseph to bring his entire family to Egypt. He had them settle in the land of Goshen, which he considered the "best part of the land." That was nice of him since allowing them to live among the Egyptians was a non-option. The Hebrew people were considered mere sheepherders, despised in Egyptian culture. Yet, that land was nothing to sneeze at, and it served them well — so well, in fact, they multiplied and prospered. But, by a couple of Pharaohs later, Israel had grown so large they were considered a political threat to the Egyptian government.

In response, the Pharaoh sought to reduce their population through hard labor and infanticide. Nothing the Egyptians did worked though. The Hebrew midwives refused to kill those precious babies, and the more the Egyptians oppressed the Hebrews, the more they multiplied and prospered.

Enter Moses

In the book of Exodus, the story continues as Moses, the deliverer of the Hebrews (Jews), was born during the time of the order to kill all the male Hebrew babies. So his mother, Jochebed, hid him in a basket among the reeds where Pharaoh's daughter found him, adopted him into the royal family, and reared him as an Egyptian prince.

Moses became a highly respected Egyptian leader (Josephus, Antiq. 2:10:1). An early indication of his calling manifested on the day his adopted mother brought him to her father, the Pharaoh. She told him she had adopted the child as heir to his throne, since there were no other heirs apparent. In an act of acceptance, Pharaoh handed his headdress to Moses, who, as if acting out a prophecy, threw, twisted, and stomped on it!

Another indication of Moses' calling occurred decades later. Around the time he visited Goshen, an Egyptian slave driver ended up taking a dirt nap in a grass blanket because Moses caught him mistreating a Hebrew slave. Moses hid the slave driver's body and went on with life thinking nobody knew about what he had done. Until, that is, the day Moses tried to break up a fight between two Hebrew slaves and was met with a hardy you've-got-a-lot-of- nerve-talking that ended with Moses becoming a fugitive from justice with an Egyptian price on his head. He ended up herding sheep in the land of Midian, where he must have been in some kind of spiritual boot camp in preparation for his inevitable destiny.

His attempts at talking God out of his appointed mission were, of course, unfruitful, and 430 years after God's promise to Abraham, Moses stepped into his destiny, leading an enslaved nation out of Egyptian bondage.

Ungrateful Nation

The children of Israel did a lot of murmuring and complaining along the way, and more than once Moses grew tired of being the scapegoat blamed for all their troubles. One day everybody was thirsty and needed to water the livestock. As usual, they started blaming Moses for dragging them into the desert to suffer. They wanted to go back to Egypt, preferring the former bondage to the present reality.

Moses took it to God, who instructed him to speak to a rock so water would spring forth. God had to know He was talking to the same man who threw the Ten Commandments against the mountain, shattering them before he ever relayed a word of them to the Israelites. So He couldn't have been surprised when Moses double-whacked the rock as he summarily blessed out the whole ungrateful lot of them.

Surprised or not, God wasn't having it. He told Moses he would never get to enter the Promised Land. Opinions differ as to exactly why God finally lost patience with Moses. Most agree the punishment seemed to far outweigh the crime. However, when you consider the back-story, it makes more sense.

The Root

The root of the matter goes back to Moses' days in the Egyptian palace. The Bible tells us two things occurred: first, Moses was led to go visit his people (the Hebrews) in Goshen; and second, he committed murder; the mixture of the two events changed the trajectory of his life. This is a chain of events that we need to look at, in succession, in order to see where exactly it all went wrong. Here is how it works:

1. The Event: Something happens
2. The Seed: Your response
3. The Harvest: Final outcome

The way the human mind works is innate to the human condition. It's prevailed since Adam and Eve. Everything we think drives how we act, so this is the framework we will use to evaluate the events leading up to Moses' first forty-year exile. First, the event, then the response (seed), and finally the outcome (harvest).

Event: The Goshen Visit

We see Moses visiting Goshen, the land where the Hebrews lived from the time of Joseph. Remember, Moses was indoctrinated in the Egyptian lifestyle. For all intent and purposes, he was a child of Pharaoh. As the crown prince of Egypt, he was in line for the Egyptian throne. He was the big man on campus, and he ruled over the Egyptian slave drivers.

Moses was Hebrew by blood but Egyptian by culture. Egyptians wouldn't even eat with a Hebrew, holding them in disdain. So for him, going to Goshen was significant. I like to think God led Moses there, and I like to think his visit spiritually unlocked or solidified his God-ordained calling. He was obviously deeply moved by what he saw. It had to have been worse than he imagined, even after seeing how they were treated on a daily basis.

Response: Seed Sown

During this visit (Exodus 2:11) Moses killed an Egyptian for mistreating a Hebrew slave. Apparently, he had a profound sense of purpose — to deliver his people. He also had a temper! The combination of his sense of calling and an apparently recurring anger management problem came together at what turned out to be a major crossroads in Moses' life. The two made for a dangerous mix that short-circuited his path to destiny. Now let's go back to the list. Take another look and see that something happened with Moses between Steps 1 and 2. What was it?

Event: Goshen visit and a slave mistreated. So far so good. No problem here.

Response: Murder; alrighty then. Looks like something went wrong between the event and the response. We need to take a closer look.

Between the event and the response is that enemy territory called the battlefield, the mind, where a subconscious system of destiny-destroying thought processes resides. When your mind is hijacked by the Defense System, anything purpose-related is on lockdown. Within mere seconds, we draw conclusions and react without the slightest consideration of the consequences. Perceptions (what we think of the event) trigger our emotions and drive how we respond. That response is a seed planted toward our own ultimate harvest.

1. **Perception of the event:** your life is the backdrop that drives how you experience an event on a mental or thought level. Everything you've been through, good and bad, are categorized using a system all your own. It colors how you process the world around you. We think about the event based on something **in** our pasts, which perpetuates emotions tied to the past. When that happens, we automatically respond as if we are in the past. With Moses, an apparently insidious anger colored how he saw the event. He saw something in Goshen that got his ire up, triggering something that was brewing under his emotional surface. That thing distorted his perception. In that moment

of anger, Moses was blind to the implications of that dynamic. His thoughts were all askew because of a tainted perspective on an event.

2. **Perspective:** the conclusions drawn from our perceptions form our perspectives (how we view the world). Say there is a rock on a conference table. Everybody who enters the room is drawn into a discussion about the rock. Nobody seems to have the same perspective on it. Some say it's beautiful because of some childhood memory. Another person thinks it should be cracked open to see if it carries some precious stone. Another person backs away because it looks unsanitary. All these are different perspectives on an inanimate object — the rock. You could move the rock, look at it differently, but it's still a rock, no matter how you see it. That's how it is when we interpret an event. Realistically, the event is what it is. How people react to it is based on their own perceptions. The anger that rose up in Moses brewed inside for who knows how long. He wore angry glasses that distorted his perceptions and twisted the conclusions he drew from them. Something he was thinking was out of whack, triggering an inappropriate emotional response.

3. **Harvest:** Whenever we are hijacked by negative thoughts, our feelings follow suit and drive us to responses. Those responses determine our outcomes or harvests. When he killed that slave driver, Moses had Mosesitus — he was blinded by anger. It wound up sidelining him for forty years. If he did not pull it together, he stood to miss the boat completely, as we will see in the second desert-forty.

These three steps hold the key to what happened to Moses. Things were good otherwise. Spiritually he sensed his calling. The Goshen visit appears to have solidified it as he was deeply moved by the profound oppression he witnessed. But when that old anger monster threw itself into the mix, it effectively short-circuited his destiny. The end result: because in a moment of reactionary passion Moses let emotion rule, *he* would never rule. In that pivotal moment, history was altered, and the entire trajectory of his life changed forever.

Harvest: Destiny Delayed

Moses was in line to become Pharaoh until he gave in to a single moment of anger that destroyed any possibility of becoming king of Egypt. It sent him into self- imposed exile, a fugitive from justice. Deep. Right? It gets deeper.

Collateral Damage

Here's the kicker: as Pharaoh, couldn't Moses have issued an edict freeing the Hebrews from bondage? Wouldn't that have been the easiest solution? Who's to say that wasn't how God initially designed the plan? As it stood, that plan was forever changed. The collateral damage is the forty years the Hebrews stayed enslaved while Moses did his first desert-forty. As you'll soon see, Moses would get many opportunities to get it right over the next eighty years.

Same Scene, Different Players

In the University of Hard Knocks you get to take the lesson over and over, if necessary, until you finally get it right. Once you do, you're prepared for the next step on the Path to Purpose. God can't afford to let you fail because you were obstinate in some area.

Note the reference to "some area." We can find obedience easier in some areas than others. Those stubborn areas cause us problems. Those areas sometimes cut so deeply we don't remember the event that perpetuated the hurt out of which we're operating. We have to be determined and focused to root out these areas and expose them to light. Otherwise, we get another go around that mountain — same scene, different players — as Moses must have learned at some point in his eighty desert years.

That Seed

Moses' response to seeing the Egyptian mistreating the Hebrew slave goes back to what is at the core of his issues. What seed is at the core of it? Though not specifically stated in Scripture, it's clear he carried a seed of anger. He was a complicated man, to be sure, because Scripture also describes him as "patient." I don't see a lot of patience in coldcocking some dude. Maybe that first desert-forty mellowed him a bit.

Moses also could have been struggling with identity issues that come with knowing you are adopted. He had to know it. From the start, it had to have been the main point of gossip. Remember, he was returned to his mother for nursing. Were there rejection issues with that whole back and forth?

He could have been teased as a child because he looked Jewish, and everybody knew he was adopted. Imagine the heckling he took from classmates and playmates. Growing up a child of the Pharaoh did little to cushion the reality of who he really was. He was Jewish, plain and simple. No matter how much Egyptian culture was drilled into him, he was Jewish by blood. Even being reared Egyptian, he could not hide it. You could look at him and see it.

As if living in a culture that held his people in disdain wasn't enough to foster a seed of anger, he could have been battling jealousy among various hopeful successors that felt no Hebrew blood should ever occupy the Egyptian throne. On the flip side, there he was directing the very slave drivers who were putting the screws to the Hebrews. How much did the children of Israel trust him? How confusing must this have been? Mr. Egyptian War Hero, the deliverer? Then he had the nerve to abscond to who knows where for how long? Could there have been rejection from that side too?

Being human, no less prone to the human condition than we are, Moses probably internalized all that rejection and started believing it on some deeper level, especially while growing up. One of the excuses he used to try to get out of leading the exodus was that he stuttered. Stuttering is a condition that can be associated with past emotional trauma. Could this be further evidence of what fueled his anger? Whatever the case, Moses must have carried the seed of that rejection and anger, in spite of a remarkable military career in Egypt, and in spite of the mission he would later face.

Whether Moses got with the program or not, this much is clear: there was a mission to be accomplished, and it was all a part of the Master Plan. Oh yes, the mission was eventually accomplished, Moses was going to do what God called him to do. God still held him accountable to fulfill his purpose. But at the hands of Mosesitus blindness, the cost would not be his alone to bear.

Mosesitus: Desert-Forty Part II

The nation of Israel began with a childless old man and woman who miraculously conceived their first child when he was over a hundred years old, and she was ninety. Okay, I know, Abraham and Sarah didn't believe it either. But true to His word, an entire nation began with the miraculous conception of their first child. If God could do that, He could surely follow through on the Promised Land.

God gave that land to Abraham's descendants as part of what's called the Abrahamic Covenants. God sealed that deal with Abraham in a ceremony that etched for eternity an unconditional and irrevocable promise. This covenant could never be broken; the parties pledged to their own responsibility to make it so. Generally, this type of ceremony required two people to walk between animal parts. But in this case, nothing was required of Abraham. God put him to sleep first. So the promise did not hang on anything Abraham could do.

A smoking furnace and a flaming torch symbolized God's presence. Since it takes two to make a covenant, I choose to believe Jesus was there with Him among those pieces, swearing to an immutable blood covenant. God does not renege on His promises. This thing was etched in eternal stone. Keep that in mind as you read along.

Fast forward a few hundred years to Israel versus Pharaoh, the end of Egyptian exile, and the desert journey. Israel was only days from realizing the promise. God's plan was an eleven-day journey across the Jordan to stake claim to every piece of ground on which they walked. Sounds simple enough, right? Think again. The quickest route out of Egypt was through Philistine territory, which meant war from which God knew the Hebrews would run.

That land was a huge deal! Other people already lived on that land when God made the promise, and they fought to keep it. They were not trying to hear about some God they didn't worship, much less give in to some cosmic order He had issued about their possession. Instead, He took them through the Red Sea, which they remarkably crossed on dry land. Then the great waters converged over their enemies. Not a single Egyptian soldier made it across alive. Not a single Hebrew was lost. What a show of unmatched might and power! You could not lose with the "stuff" God used, and from one enemy kingdom to the other, everybody knew it. Well, not everybody. Even after crossing the Red Sea in that miraculous display of God's power, the group was sidelined.

When it was time to take that first bit of land, their mentalities short-circuited the plan.

The Mission

The original plan also never included forty wandering years in a dry desert. That little stint was compliments of more than a few negative attitudes. This was never more evident than when they reached Canaan's border. In the let's-do- this-our-own- way department, the people decided it was better to investigate what they were up against than to take the land by force as God instructed. The suggestion sounded good to Moses, so he issued specific instructions, including the reconnaissance route and intelligence they were to gather.

The whole idea was unnecessary since God had already told them it flowed with milk and honey. They had been hearing that story for centuries. He had already given them the land, and an Egyptian war hero with national acclaim to lead them. Israel had waited centuries for that day. Their ancestors died with the hope of the promise coursing through their spiritual veins. But instead of taking the land as instructed, they wanted more proof.

Just the Facts

Forty days later the search party returned with the long-awaited report. They carried with them pomegranates, figs, and a single cluster of grapes so huge they had to carry them from a pole stretched between them. These are the facts as reported. Everybody heard the same thing at the same time, and nobody could claim any monkey business, because each tribe had a representative in the search party (See Numbers 13:28–29):

- The land surely flows with milk and honey; and this is the fruit of it.
- The people are strong that dwell in the land, the cities walls are great.
- We saw the children of Anak.
- The Amalekites dwell in the land of the south; the Hittites, Jebusites, and Amorites dwell in the mountains.
- The Canaanites dwell by the sea and along the Jordan.

Those are the facts as recorded, just straight up facts, no fluff. Now let's rejoin the story where we find Caleb addressing the crowd.

Note that he "stilled the people." My guess is they were already complaining, having drawn their own conclusions. Let's look at how they interpreted the report.

Interpretation: Everybody's "Fake" On It

For purposes of my translation of Scripture, let's say they are murmuring when Caleb speaks up: "*Don't believe them! I was there! The land is really flowing with milk and honey. Let's go. We've got this. These Yahoos are no match for us! What are we waiting for? Come on, you guys. Let's do this!*"

The Negative Nellies argue back, "*Yeah, it's flowing with milk and honey. But, dude! Have you lost your ever-loving mind? We're no match for them. We're going to get clobbered! No way!*"

Some facts are irrefutable. Even the naysayers admitted to seeing exactly what God had said they would. But in the face of that reality, they chose to believe something different, even to the point of being ridiculous. They insisted Canaan was a land that eats up its inhabitants. Okay, now we've got *Cannibal* Land? This is getting out of hand.

Come on, how can the land be plentiful (as evidenced by the fruit they brought back) *and* eat up its inhabitants (who are apparently eating so well their size is a point of fear)? It seems to me we just heard of several groups of people who lived in Canaan. Where are the victims of this eat-'em-up land, and where was that in the list of facts they reported? We now have a major contradiction in interpretation, the cause for which is glimpsed in their next statement. Again, this is my correlation:

"*These people are huge. Shoot, we're insects next to those sons of Anak. We had to look like grasshoppers to them!*"

There it is. In their own sight, those men saw themselves as grasshoppers shadowed at the feet of giants. And that's how they believed others saw them. Because of how they were treated under bondage, this is the only way they could see themselves. Mosesitus blinded by the bondage of the past, they were suspicious and distrustful of anything outside of their own tainted points of view. Clueless and caught up, they fell into the age-old mind game that diverts focus from anything destiny related.

Reality check! How did they know what the inhabitants thought of them? The mission was covert. Did those eat-'em-up giants in a self-devouring land ever even see them? No, not likely. The naysayers assumed the opinion of the inhabitants based on their own self-perceptions. Now here's the clincher: rather than considering that their perceptions were ill conceived, they chose to contradict God's direction. They allowed misperception to drive every conclusion they drew of the same facts from which Caleb and Joshua determined otherwise.

At that point, the people had a choice to make. They had the facts and two interpretations before them. Joshua and Caleb said they could take the land. The Negative Nellies interpreted the same facts as, "*No way can we beat those giants with our grasshopper hinnies!*" Destiny swung in the balance.

Response: Seed Sown

Nobody got any sleep that night because they cried all night. Contrition wasn't the issue. You have to know you *have* a problem to recognize you *are* the problem. No, no. They spent the night fussing about Moses, Aaron, and God Himself. They were whining about how they were about to die in the wilderness, how much better they'd had it in Egypt, and how wrong it was to lead them into the wilderness to die. They planned a coup to get rid of Moses and elect somebody to take them back to Egypt. Never mind the oppressive slavery they were under with that regime. Despite wondrous provision and guidance, their flawed thinking was impenetrable.

Seeing the huge mistake they were making, Moses and Aaron fell on their faces before God as Joshua and Caleb tried again to talk sense into the relentless crowd. To no avail, they pleaded with the people to stop rebelling. There was no getting through to them. Just as they were getting ready to stone Joshua and Caleb to death, God showed up. How much more can I do? That did it! You're about to get exactly what your mouths called for. You are mind bent on believing anything but Me, and I've had it!

Can you imagine? Cloud by day, flaming pillar by night, food falling from the sky, clothes didn't wear out, no sickness. In the face of all that, plus the Red Sea crossing, there He stood having to call them out for rebellious disobedience, murmuring, and complaining. He was about to disinherit them and let them all die by a plague. But true to form, Moses reminded God of His merciful nature, and He acquiesced. All good, but the consequences still lay in wait.

Harvest: Destiny Redirected

After putting up with it ten times, God had had enough. This was their sentence:

> *Because those who have seen My glory and My miracles and have [tested me] ten times, and have not [listened], not one of them will ever see the land I promised. No one who has treated me with contempt will ever see it. (See Numbers 14:20–23.)*

Oh my goodness! God held them in contempt for disobedience and obstinacy. He had steadily shown Himself strong on their behalf, and they gave Him this? To me He sounds insulted, angry, and fed up.

The ten negative men died by a plague anyway, and when the news spread that God was turning the whole nation away from the Promised Land, they mourned and asked for forgiveness, but it was too late. God didn't have to look far for an appropriate sentence for the rest of the disbelievers. Their words were their condemnation. Their attitudes, their judgment: *"As sure as I live . . . as you have spoken . . . so will I do to you: Your carcasses shall fall in this wilderness... you shall not come into the land"* (vv. 28–30). Because ten out of twelve of the search party disbelieved firsthand eyewitness accounts in support of the promise, relayed that disbelief to the people, and refused to relent, a whole nation paid the consequences.

Collateral Damage

The destiny of the Hebrews was short-circuited, not by the event but by their response to it. Their choices held the entire Hebrew nation hostage to a forty- year holding pattern! Forty years they would have to wander the wilderness until all the murmuring complainers bit the dust. They wrote their own fates by repeated expressions of the negativity that festered in their hearts.

Picture it. There stood God Himself between the children of Israel and the Promised Land. Before Him a defiant nation stood within arm's reach of a dream they could not see. They were Mosesitus blinded by their own fear and disbelief, carried forward out of bondage. The result was constant rebellion and disregard for their leaders and God. The rebellion was so deeply engrained that their mourning wasn't out of repentance or contrition. Contrition would not have found them getting right up the next morning and attacking Canaan anyway. They rebelliously rushed into battle over the objection of the Commander-in-Chief.

Moses told them not to do it. I can just hear him saying, "*What part of 'you blew it' don't you guys get?*" They got clobbered — people died at the hands of their own rebellion, and the entire Hebrew nation still had to roam the desert wilderness for another forty years.

At the Core

There's still something sticking in my craw here. Did you catch it? Why was nobody talking about that fruit? Clearly, grapes that size were unusual. Why was that clear evidence of abundance completely ignored? Everybody agreed the land was just as God had described it. The evidence was there for all to see.

Why wasn't the sight of that fruit enough to convince them that the battle was well worth the effort? Why is it that, when the ten spread the evil report that the land ate up its inhabitants, the sight of the fruit didn't open their eyes? How can a land that ate up its inhabitants produce such huge fruit? Nobody of the *carcass group* found it significant. They were determined to see it their own way. They were afraid of war. Nothing God, Moses, or Aaron did would change that. We are left with a bunch of people, carcasses strewn across the desert floor, and I'm guessing most of them died still not understanding why they were not allowed to enter. Some of them probably died still blaming God, Moses, and Aaron for the failure.

It is easier to judge them than to apply the lesson to ourselves. We are so far removed we sometimes think these are just stories or that the "characters," because they're in the Bible, had some supernatural abilities. It's easy to wonder why, in the face of all these miracles, they just could not believe God.

They were human beings, folks, just plain human beings living in extraordinary times. They lived, they died, they bled, they cried, just as we do. After over two hundred years of multigenerational bondage, suddenly the land they thought was home, no longer was. The Pharaoh with whom they had favor was long gone by then. The current Pharaoh didn't know Joseph from Adam's housecat, and he felt no obligation to any promises his predecessor made to Joseph. The days of peace ended abruptly. Suddenly the Hebrews were no longer welcome in Egypt, the only home they knew. Maybe some of them considered the promise just a fairy tale. They saw so many generations come and go while waiting, they might have gotten comfortable with the status quo.

Think how they must have felt when Moses absconded for forty years? If they believed him to be the deliverer, they had to be confused, disappointed, and angry when they heard he had murdered somebody and gone into hiding. Even without the whole Mosesitus issue, trusting *him* had to be a challenge.

Destiny Denied

The children of Israel were blinded by a form of Mosesitus grounded in decades of oppression. Imagine the bitterness that must have festered in their souls at the cruel hands of the Egyptian slave masters? That they prospered and multiplied in spite of it doesn't mean they didn't bear the physical and emotional scars of that oppression. That trauma cut deeper with each lash of the whip. It took a fatal toll as, along with the riches they carried out of Egypt, they carried the fear-soaked remnants of generations of bondage. Equipped and well able or not, they were prone to the negativity that rendered all of it of no effect.

Here's the upshot: having a purpose, calling, a mission, and being equipped to execute it, doesn't guarantee we will realize our own Promised Land or even recognize it when we see it before us. Israel stood at its border and never stepped foot on it. Those who did make it, didn't magically own it. They had to fight their way through, claiming it one battle at a time. They won some, they lost some. The losses were always at the hands of their own disobedience. The ease or difficulty of their journey was in direct relation to their degree of obedience or obstinacy. It depended on what side of God they were. So, while war was inevitable, the losses were unnecessary.

The Hebrews had a slave mentality, another form of Mosesitus. No matter how far from Egypt they got, their minds were still in bondage to the past. The outcome was that their attitudes, decisions, and behaviors seeded a harvest opposite of what God intended. It is the same outcome Adam and Eve received — the complete opposite of what God intended. Destiny didn't deny them. They denied destiny.

Decision and Destiny

This is not the stuff of fairy tales. Those people really stood face to face with a promise God had made to the father of their existence. They knew of the promise. The story was a part of their culture. That is the uniqueness of the Jewish people — their race is their culture and their religion. The Promised Land was their heritage, and to this day, it's part of who they are. In spite of all that, the same set of facts was interpreted two different ways, with two different outcomes. Two hundred ten years of bondage had taken their toll, and the rebellion it birthed blinded them.

They were victims of stolen vision. They forgot who they were. They saw themselves as slaves in bondage, and on some strange level, they had become comfortable with it. Yes, they wanted out of it, there's no doubt, just as I wanted out of my cycle of relationship doom. But to get there they had to break through the mental bondage. It stood between them and the promise. It stood between them and God. It stood between them and destiny.

Stolen Focus, Stolen Vision

The carcass group fell prey to a mindset that might have served them well during slavery, but it was completely maladaptive during the Exodus. They were so full of everything that went before, they couldn't fathom freedom or see the error of their perspectives. They had learned utter distrust for their Egyptian oppressors, an attitude they carried into their post-bondage lives. It distorted how they perceived reality. It drove how they related to God-ordained leadership and to God Himself.

They were rebellious to the bone because of a defensive armor of distrust and bitterness that was so entrenched they were blinded to any reality to the contrary (the fruit). It's the perpetual human condition. We are all prone to these blind spots, and we all blindly fall into poor choices and behaviors born out of unrealistic thinking.

Living in the Past

As I wrote this, I was watching the funeral of Whitney Houston. That one was especially tough for me. I thought about her daily. It was as if she was hovering somewhere inside. I don't understand it other than to say that, for the first time, I felt the sweetness of Whitney's spirit. My heart broke for Cissy Houston, for whom every gut-wrenching, soul-rending, ounce of grief was painfully etched in her expression. She barely withstood the buckling strain of burying her baby girl. There aren't words. Then there was Whitney's daughter, Bobbi Kristina, who stayed on my mind as I wondered how such a young woman could possibly withstand such a burden of grief, the immeasurable loss of her mother, her friend. It was hard to even *think* about it. At the time, the last thing I could have imagined is that Bobbi Kristina would soon suffer a death very similar to that of her mother.

Contrary to the national media, Whitney's drug use was an inappropriate focus. What broke my heart was the unbearable pain that must have fueled it. What was hurting her so deeply? That was what went through me as I reflected on her inimitable talent, her beauty, and a voice only the heart and hands of God could have crafted. The world may never know what haunted that stately woman who exuded such class and dignity. To my knowledge, she never spoke about it publicly. I'm convinced it was partly what drove her to fame and fortune, while simultaneously fueling the very public challenges in her personal life. What was evident from the expressions of those who memorialized her is that she was steadfast in her faith. She never wavered in her love for God, and she clearly ran to Him, never allowing whatever she was going through to keep her from the God she loved. Whitney's unquenchable spirit demonstrated the resilience that drove her to fame. Yet, her life was colored by something so deep it eventually led to our losing her. She is not alone.

There are a lot of us stuffing things out of shame, guilt, or other fear- based thoughts born out of painful life experiences. We ignore it, but as long as we are still driven by that hurt, we're operating from a victim mentality. That Whitney excelled in her God-given talents, right in the middle of the mess, speaks volumes for her determination and focus. However, I wonder how different her life would have been had she coupled that resounding determination with the realization of her own power to choose a different outcome.

The past creeps in when least expected, and we are unaware that we are barely functioning in our purpose. As long as the past has a hold on us, we are slaves, chained and shackled to what went before.

Chained

We have heard sermons with all their wonderful promises of beauty for ashes, running the race, and having the mind of Christ. But what exactly does all that mean in the real world? "Running the race" means staying focused on the goal, the vision, and the desired outcome. Every time runners look anywhere but forward, they lose time. That fraction of a second can mean victory or disappointment. "Beauty for ashes" means when your back's against the wall, and all seems lost, victory, celebration, and joy await you. Summed up, they both mean this: destiny hasn't changed or moved. It is waiting on you! To get there takes something other than your human mind. To get there takes tapping into unchanging truth. It takes tapping into the Mind of Christ.

This is a bit confusing considering He had two sides, so to speak. He was all God and all man, so He apparently tapped into His God side to triumph over his human mind. The human mind of Jesus was as spiritually useless to Him as ours is to us. We already have the Mind of Christ by that standard. So this has to be talking about the way He leveraged His spiritual side to bring His human mind in line with truth. Jesus already knew the human mind couldn't understand God or fathom anything about Him. Counting on *it* is a waste of time. We know that the Commander-in-Chief has the war plan and a fail-proof strategy to navigate enemy mindfields. It's going to take a change of our human minds to find our way back to who we really are.

It took me a long time to get that. During the crisis that spurred writing this book, I was dealing with the residual effects of abortion, rape, molestation, and domestic violence. I was so caught-up I never realized I was going through life reacting to things – Kneejerk Jessie! Living that reactionary existence did not afford time to stop, turn around, and process through the fallout. Consequently, each painful experience was heaped upon another. I went through two marriages in that condition. After the second, I decided to chill out. I would park the car Friday afternoon and didn't come out of the house again until Monday morning. It worked for me. I was comfortable, and I didn't have to deal with anybody's drama. At first, it was a time for healing and self-evaluation. A few years into it, though, it came to me that I was self-isolating out of fear. I preferred the comfort of past relationships. It was a way of hiding from the future. As long as I stayed with what I knew, there would be no surprises, no being blindsided. That cloak of fear was my safe zone.

Eventually, I couldn't take another bout of reacting to one event after another without a game plan for navigating the obstacle course that was my life. Isolation was just a bandage on a gaping wound. It was nothing more than fooling myself into some false sense of control. It took a lot of deliberate discipline to stop running, face truth about the matter, and trust God to walk me through the fear that drove my isolation. At that point, I had no clue how to change it. But I refused to go another round with the same old status quo. I was embarking on a phase the Bible calls "growth work."

> *Don't be misled: No one makes a fool of God. What a person plants, he will harvest. The person who plants selfishness, ignoring the needs of others – ignoring God harvests a crop of weeds. All he'll have to show for his life is weeds! But the one who plants in response to God, letting God's Spirit do the growth work in him, harvests a crop of real life, eternal life (MSG) (Galatians 6:7-8).*

Note that the words, growth work, imply a process. It clearly says that growth occurs within as we allow God to work the kinks out of our characters. Work is right. Sometimes we go along with it kicking and screaming. Nevertheless, God honors us as we trust and honor Him. However, the promise is conditioned on the growth. There is no "out" clause in this. Moses didn't get a pass, and neither did the children of Israel.

Moses died in the desert along with the carcass group because he, too, was caught up in the Mosesitus madness. He spent two-thirds of his life in the desert. The first time was in preparation for the mission. After eliminating that slave master, it was off to the desert for him! The second time was during the mission, because the same old anger issues that drove him to murder were still out of control.

It's the hidden areas of our emotions that become prime targets on the battlefield. They are crippling burdens. They are distractions from purpose. There is no room on Purpose Road for dead weight, and until it's unloaded, the journey will be difficult at best.

Dead Weight

Roman literature describes King Mezentius, a king so diabolical he didn't even honor the gods. The Romans had their pick of gods, depending on the situation. That none of them suited *his* taste reveals a deeply rebellious nature. Of Mezentius, it is written, "He ruled . . . with arrogant power and savage weaponry." Arrogant is an understatement. This man made up rules as he went along. Imagine living under the rule of a man *without* rule. He was a diabolical dude. He even tied corpses to people as torture, "*placing hand on hand and face against face,*" killing them by a slow "*lingering death, in that wretched embrace, that ooze of disease and decomposition.*"[1]

Think about the mirror image that evokes. With a corpse tied to you hand to hand, face to face, as if lying flat against a mirror, you have no mobility — none. You had better hope you are lying down when they do it because you're stuck right there in the same position as the dead guy . . . for the duration. You can't eat. The smell probably makes getting any sleep a thing of the past. You're left to rot along with that corpse, a mirror image of your own slow, inevitable, demise.

Fake-enstein: Who Do You Think You Are?

In this analogy, the corpse is our past. Gone! Done! Just like the corpse, it's dead. You can't bring it back. It's dead weight, pure and simple. Our thoughts are the chains that bind us to this body of death. We tell ourselves over and over again the same bitter stories from the past. Just like being chained to a corpse, nothing short of breaking that chain will free us. Meanwhile, a glimpse in the mirror reflects the rotten corpses of our pasts. It's all we see.

We don't see our True Selves because we've taken on the rotten, stinking, pieces of other people's dead weight. Generally, the people who hurt us are strapped to the corpses of their own pasts. Every hurt that they inflict on us is tantamount to their slinging rotten flesh from their own corpses. As we internalize these wrongs by lack of forgiveness, bitterness, fear, anger, etc., they become embedded into our souls creating a defensive force field (defense system) that repels truth. Our souls become impermeable to anything destiny-related as denial blinds us (Mosesitus) to facing or seeing what has morphed us out of our True Selves.

As we develop this Fake-enstein persona, we become a pieced together conglomerate of all the rotten corpses of every sorry individual that ever hurt us. With every wrong we take on a little of the offender until we become mutated into the complete opposites of our

True Selves. Then it creates a system of lies and fear to repel the truth that will free us as we begin to see ourselves as one with these corpses of the

Morpheus Fake-Enstein

past. It's all a crafty system of Fake-en*lies* created when we internalize wrongs. Nobody sees who we really are because all we're projecting is this bogus conglomeration of stinking lies! Just as Israel was turned back from the Promised Land, we're Mosesitus blind to anything that contradicts our own realities. We have gotten used to the smell of that rot. Just like the Hebrews, we're mentally bound. We must avoid the end they met. They preferred the former bondage to the promise. They were chained to the past they left behind. They found solace in the scent of that bondage and took comfort in its familiarity. They saw themselves as one with it, and they couldn't see the destiny before them.

A Million Faces of *Fake*-enstein

There are a million versions of Frankenstein, and there are a million faces of Old Fakey. Whatever version you choose, they are all pieced together from corpses, nothing matching, stitches and all. My favorite is the one with the huge bolt through his neck. It ought to be through his head. That's where Fake-enstein sets up forces. He lives there and plans to rule his domain. His game is weak but effective as he smugly morphs our true personalities into whatever it takes to trip us up. If our God-given character is kind and mild, he will morph us into overbearing, inconsiderate people.

If we are assertive, he will morph us into wallflowers. Fakey's main game is keeping things out of balance. It takes keen discernment to catch him at it because he comes with so many disguises. Sometimes he will morph our good traits until they are overboard. Way over the top. It will go to one extreme or the other. Whatever way we morph, we might still get glimpses of our True Selves. We might even experience some level of success, but as long as Old Fakey is in the mix, it can be nothing like what God intended.

I, too, had spiritually lucid moments when I operated in my purpose. But the cussing, fit-prone woman I was had to be dealt with before God could effectively and consistently trust me in the mission. I could have been preaching at the top of my lungs with everybody's full attention, and it never could have made the airwaves because they would have had to bleep every third word to get past the censors. I was dichotomy personified as occasionally the real me sneaked past my defenses before I would jump back into Mr. Hyde mode, hoping nobody would notice that glimpse of Dr. Jekyll lurking in the shadows. If more good than harm was done, it was by God's grace and glory alone.

The whole time I had no idea what had happened to me. I just went with the emotional flow, regardless of the situation or circumstance. Most of the time I had no idea how my overall demeanor was off-putting or how uncomfortable others were around me. A supervisor once described me as "unapproachable." Of course, it peeved me because I was stuck in denial. She was right, though. I was volatile, unpredictable, unapproachable, and I couldn't have cared less. I was fine in my blindness, and I wasn't going to hear any truth without a fight.

Just as thoughts are the chains that bind us to our pasts, Mosesitus (denial) is the blindfold that keeps us from seeing that we are bound. As I discovered from writing this book, truth has a way of blindsiding us when least expected. I had been experiencing writer's block and didn't know why I couldn't get back into the manuscript. That happened several times during the seven years over which I was writing. Each time it was because there was another level of healing I had to reach before I could move forward. The following experience was one of the most profound.

Queen of Denial

After leaving my abusive first husband with nothing but the nightgown on my back, in the throes of a nervous breakdown, and nowhere to go, I was denied residency at the local domestic violence center because my third shift job went past their curfew. As I went from pillar to post looking for a place to stay, I eventually landed at a local motel. I always had breakfast at the restaurant next door. There I met a man and invited him over. Dumb move! He eventually left without a word as I lay sodomized, raped, and bleeding on the bed. From the beginning of the incident to the end I was at the rapist's mercy, and believe me, he had no mercy.

Once it was over, I sucked it up and moved on, or so I fooled myself into thinking. I didn't know I was chained to that man's unrelenting grip because, once it was over, I failed to separate the evil I endured from who I am. Consequently, the experience and I became one (Fake-enstein). I never spoke of it in any detail. Few knew I had ever been raped. Until one day as my boyfriend, Marcus, and I were talking, it just came up and out. I don't remember why I finally spilled all the gory details exactly as they had happened, no cleaning it up, and no leaving anything out. I'll never forget his response. As we walked from the carport he asked, *"Did you go to the doctor?"*

That question was such a shock. It stopped me in my tracks. Before even getting a grip on the question, every bit of shock flew out in my tone. "Yeah," came faintly, almost whimsically as it gave away the fact that, until he asked, it had never crossed my mind. I thought, "Why didn't I go to the doctor?" In thirty years, it had never crossed my mind to get help. Suddenly Fake-enstein took over. With major attitude I remember blurting out, *"Why would I go to a doctor just to have to tell him I did something that stupid? I made the choice. I paid the consequences.*" That ended that conversation right away.

After holding his tongue for weeks, Marcus finally confronted me with, "*Linda, you talk as if you deserved what happened. You didn't ask for that. You didn't deserve it. They have to own what they did to you.*" My problem, he pointed out, was that I think more as a man than a woman. He explained that if little girls run to mom or dad when they get hurt, they are comforted and allowed to cry. They are taught to allow emotion and to generally reach out to others when they need support.

Conversely, he said, when a little boy gets hurt and runs to daddy, he isn't socialized to spend a whole lot of time in his emotions. He might get a pat on the head from daddy and told to man-up. So whenever something went wrong, I jumped into scripted behavior: Man-up! Suck it up! Get up! Get on with it! You big baby! If you hadn't been there, you wouldn't have had to go through that, big dummy. It's nobody's fault but your own. As unreasonable as that *you-made-your-bed-so-lie-in-it* perspective was, to me it was the truth by which I lived. I had no clue there was any other way of thinking about it.

Eventually I figured out that I had internalized the experience as if I deserved to be raped. Until that moment, I had not seen that I didn't deserve to be raped just because I made a poor decision. Yes, I was in that place at that time of my own volition. But that *man* chose to rape me. I didn't ask him to. I had no clue he was a rapist.

From the beginning of the event until he let me go, I was at his mercy. Once it was over, I failed to separate the evil done *to* me, from who I am. Consequently, the experience and I became one and he may as well have kept me in his unrelenting grip for the next thirty years. For thirty years, an inner loathing drove me. Out of it came myriad other issues leading to wrong relationships and cyclical hurt. Each time I figured I had to suck it up, woman-up, and move on to the next trauma. It left no room to face up to or acknowledge the pain. It allowed indefinite avoidance, and it strengthened an irrational belief system I didn't even know I had. I was so ashamed of myself for putting myself in that position.

You know you have a blind spot when, in the aftermath of an emotional hijacking, you wonder, "What in the world was that?" and "Where did that come from?" In hindsight, my first clue should have been years prior when my second husband asked me about the incident.

All he knew was that I had been raped. I had never related any details about it. He simply asked, *"When that guy raped you, did you let him in?"*

Boy, if that hadn't been before the 9/11 attacks, they would have called out the troops. I remember a force rushing up inside me as the lie flew out my mouth, *"No!"* The tone let him know never to touch that subject again, and I went on my merry, blind way. Even after that reaction, I had no idea it was rotting inside me. It would be over a decade later that the conversation with Marcus would shock me to my spiritual senses and recalibrate my entire course. That day I took another step of healing along my Path of Purpose. It put me back on track with destiny, and I set about writing again.

Immobilized

The spiritual decay we get from internalizing and acting out of damaging or painful experiences is similar to Virgil's graphic description of the Mezentius Torture. Written some nineteen centuries before Paul, the legend of King Mezentius could have been the backdrop for Paul's famous Body of Death passage in which he "described the thoughts and impulses that war[ed] within him."[2] His anguish was highlighted as he cried, *"What a wretched man I am! Who will rescue me from this body of death?"* (Romans 7:24 NKJV).

Many say "body of death" refers to sin. For our purposes, the Body of Death (corpse) is whatever negative or painful life events we still carry around, consciously or subconsciously. It's whatever trauma or painful occurrences we have internalized and held onto through defense and denial. Just as that corpse immobilized the tortured, holding on to the past immobilizes us emotionally and spiritually. It immobilizes any aspect of executing our part in the Master Plan. It shouts down purpose and short-circuits destiny. Paul struggled throughout his ministry with these thoughts and behaviors about which he was keenly aware. Unfortunately, not all of us are.

Ignorance is the path by which this leakage of our pasts sidetracks our careers, creativity, talents, and relationships. It locks down creativity at its very core. Its immobilizing grip insidiously holds us back as its tentacles bore into every aspect of our lives, summarily morphing us into anything and everything opposite to who we really are. Even in the face of consequences, we blindly amble through life, oblivious to the rotten, stinky mess bubbling below the surface.

Everybody else smells it. They are looking at us wondering what our problem is. Doesn't she smell that? Pew! Meanwhile we're looking back at them with accusatory eyes, declaring how often we are misunderstood, apologizing for the umpteenth time about saying or doing the wrong thing or licking our wounds from hurt feelings. It's everybody else's fault. What's their problem?

It's the same old blame game that started in the Garden of Eden. Nobody's owning their own choices because they are so busy focusing on anything and everything they can't control. To turn that focus inside would upset the status quo — the Defense System, which is our so-called protection from whatever pain we've internalized. Its misdirected focus and another enemy mind game to keep us duped and distracted. Stolen focus is stolen vision. Stolen vision is usurped purpose, and unfulfilled purpose equals unrealized destiny.

In Fake-enstein mode, it's not going to happen, my friend. As long as our perceptions are off, *we're* off and likely headed in the wrong direction. We are so blinded by the deception that we can't see that we are holding the key to unlock the chains that bind us to that Body of Death. Like Dorothy (There's no place like home) we, too, hold the ruby-slippers power to stop the Mosesitus madness. We are stuck in a time warp, repeating the same scene over and over, too caught up to notice the big red Out Button on the wall beside us. It's flashing neon red, and we don't see it because we're too caught up and immobilized.

Nevertheless, the repercussions are ours to bear as those connected to us in the Master Plan wait for what God wants to channel through us. Don't get me wrong, the Master Plan will go forward because God keeps His word. But it will be a lot harder on us in the long run, if we stay stuck, immobilized, and incapacitated for duty.

Bulls-Eye! Soul Connection

I used to think that because we're created in God's image we actually look like God. But when you follow that logic, you have to wonder how one Being can look like every person. While He could definitely do so if He wanted to, I think our likeness to Him is different. So I took it in a different direction.

God created us in His own image, and Adam came to life by the breath of God. If by breathing into Adam's body God imparted His Spirit — His life force — and if our spirits are clothed in our souls, then it stands to reason that one aspect in which we mirror God is our threefold existence. Just as God is Father, Son, and Holy Spirit, we are body, soul, and spirit. Our bodies are the earth suits we need to wear in order to function on earth. When we die we leave the earth gear behind.

You can look at the soul as the middle layer that floats between the body and spirit. It will gravitate toward the body (human desires and frailties) or it will gravitate toward our spirit (life force), our main connection with God. If our soul gravitates toward our bodies, it caters to our human proclivities, which include all the stinking thinking that comes with dragging around Fake-enstein. In that condition, our souls don't prosper because they have been morphed into the complete opposite of who we need to be to meet our purpose. We are severed from the very source that links us to our destinies, because we have to be our True Selves to effectively accomplish our purpose, calling, and mission. When our souls gravitate toward the Spirit, they draw supernatural strength from our connection with God. Through our spirits, we tap into His character, including His higher thoughts and plans for us. We tap into the Master Plan.

The enemy targets the soul with extreme prejudice. Cripple us there and we're on lockdown because on every conceivable level we prosper only to the degree that our souls prosper (3 John 1:2). From this standpoint, it's a wise battle strategy that takes little energy on his part. Let's look at the anatomy of the soul to see why the enemy has chosen it as his main point of attack.

Anatomy of the Soul

The soul is the epicenter of how we live. It's a repository of our lives as each experience is filed away and categorized as either good or bad. It remembers based on the emotions or feelings we attached to past events. It remembers whether we remember or not. We act according to what's stored in that repository.

Consisting of mind, will, and emotion, everything we do is filtered through our souls. Our *attitudes, perceptions, perspectives*, the *lies* we believe, and the resulting *expectations* (APPLE) are all affected by what's filed away here. This is where Fake- enstein thrives. Since we know that the mind is the battlefield, we'll discuss it first.

Mind. What goes on in the mind directs will and emotion. It makes sense from a strategic standpoint that this is a primary target.

Attack here and our will and emotions will follow. Our minds aren't subject to God's law. It's through our spirits that we relate to God. That, my friend, is why the human mind is open to enemy attack. It's fair game for the enemy. It will always be the warzone because the enemy knows the rules allow his attack at this, the weakest or the strongest aspect of our characters.

As goes the mind, so goes the soul. As goes the soul, so goes our health and life. Health and life are part of that harvest we have to cultivate to accomplish our assigned calling, purpose, and mission. God's Creative Purpose includes all three. Add them up and you have destiny!

Will. Just as the Tree of Life and the Tree of the Knowledge of Good and Evil stood in the middle of the Garden of Eden, so the will stands between the mind and emotion, and with good reason. A chain is only as strong as its weakest link, and the will is where that chain of thoughts that bind us in our pasts is broken or strengthened. Every choice is an act of our will. Just like Adam and Eve, we're free to choose destiny or disappointment.

Emotions. Emotions drive how we respond to life events. The root of the word is motion. Emotions move us to action. They drive our behaviors and how we respond to the world around us. This can be good or bad. There is nothing wrong with emotion in itself. It is a God given dynamic. Even Jesus felt happiness, sorrow, pain. So we cannot ascribe the good thing God intended as wholly wrong or bad. What we must achieve is the ability to discern our emotions so that they aren't running us; but we are in control of them. That takes rooting out the causes of negative reactions (driven by emotional attachment to the past) by addressing them at their core. We need to understand into what past event the negative emotion is rooted.

If emotions are attached to a painful past, that's how they are filed away in our souls. If that filing system is off (Fake-enstein), so are our behaviors. Let's say somebody offends you. The actual event itself might have been completely innocent as observed by others. But you are highly offended, whether anybody else agrees or not.

Looking back through the soul files, you will likely find a long- forgotten folder. Blowing off the dust, you see something's out of whack. The event in the folder is mislabeled. Instead of the label saying "Joy," it says "Hurt." Once you get everything in order, you wonder what the hoopla was about all these years! Once that label is placed on the correct emotional folder, you begin to realign your thinking. From that new perspective, you recognize that your perception of the event at hand was off kilter.

Sometimes we have to detach those emotional labels from the behavior folder in order to flip the script on Fake-enstein. When emotions are misplaced or misfiled, we don't know we are acting out of our lying pasts, so we consistently reap the only thing that seed (behavior) can yield — more of the same sorry, sad, and hurtful crop. Bottom line: Keep Fake-enstein out of the file room!

We always want our souls to gravitate toward our spirits because, through the spirit, we have relationship with God. It's through that dynamic interaction that we find the benchmark for changing old ways that hold us back from purpose. Once you get wind of some of these lying mind games, you will appreciate a standard of truth by which to navigate enemy mindfields.

Mindfields

In the course of my studies, I learned about the concepts of schema and scripts. Okay, I read it. At the time, I didn't get it. After getting my master's degree, I didn't give it another thought until I saw it play out in my own life. Then what I thought was an over complication of what must have been an otherwise simple concept, made perfect sense. Rejecting the very phenomena I personified was ironic. The shambled mess in my life came from irrational briefs I'd concocted. The same old voices told the same old Fake-enlies. As those lies became the course I navigated, my life became a reflection of them. In the aftermath of divorce, a nervous breakdown, years of self-isolation, and again making the wrong choices, I finally wised up.

It's a Scheme

Irrational beliefs are rooted in fear. From that root, fear produces thoughts, emotions, and behaviors after its own kind. Consequently, we perpetuate the very things we fear. It's a scheme designed to avert our focus to any and everything other than what matters: purpose and destiny. Schema, simply stated, describes the system of thought that informs our frames of reference, our perceptions. We filter information through this mental framework. If the framework is off, we come to believe what isn't truth about the world around us and ourselves.

With irrational schema, we are filtering the world through falsehoods we have taken on as a result of lies we are told by others or lies we have told ourselves. For example, if someone has a negative reinforcement style that hammers someone with negative messages, especially during childhood, that person will take on those negative messages as their own. They will believe the lies because they have been stamped onto their life-lenses (perspectives). Once they take on those lies, they see themselves that way, and it becomes so entrenched they reject any encouragement, messages, and information to the contrary.

That framework is so engrained and so rigid we ignore or dismiss anything that counters it. Consequently, we ignore reality in favor of information that presents little or no challenge to them. As we become the lies we have told ourselves, we behave, in any situation, based on those beliefs. We have to constantly challenge our thinking to recalibrate the falsehoods that have become rooted in our souls. This root system distorts reality as we develop distorted and irrational themes (scripts). The scheme fools us into decisions that contradict purpose and short-circuit or destroy our ultimate destinies.

Imagine a maze of twisted piping. You will see connectors and joints, spigots, and faucets. All pipe systems have cut-off valves to redirect or stop the flow in emergencies or during repairs. Yet, no matter how efficient the original design (purpose), no matter what the designer (God) intended, any blockage renders the entire system ineffective. The overall purpose is defeated as crucial sections corrode, some of the valves are stuck in the off position, and the overloaded sections have sprung leaks. If you get enough of this going on, the entire system goes into lockdown. Nothing gets in, and what comes out is tainted with fragments of the blockage (past). The more junk clogs the system, the more rigid and resistant it becomes. That's what happens to our souls when we are morphed out of our True Selves as God created us.

We have to be our True Selves to fulfill our roles in the Master Plan. By internalizing (taking it personally, focusing on retaliation, nurturing bitterness, anger, fear, and other negative emotions that become a part of us) we render ineffective or severely hinder our God-given tools to fulfill our purpose. Because we are created with all we need specific to that goal, any mutation of our True Self results in a major malfunction.

With each painful or traumatic experience, we build up soul scars (the pipe clog). Each scar contains the emotions we attach to the experience. This sets up a spiritual infection that oozes with festering emotions. When we ignore the infection, it turns into a hard, crusty, and impermeable defensive shield that hardens our hearts. Our minds, wills, and emotions are all held prisoner to its whims. We become as rigid as wood, no more than emotional Pinocchios jerked around at the behest of situation and circumstance. God, as our cosmic Geppetto, crafted us with the greatest love and care. Yet, just like Pinocchio, we kick against and run from reality until our little wooden feet catch fire. Every time we come out fighting, blindly kicking at the very source of our existence. Yet, being the loving Creator He is, God replaces them with lovingly crafted feet with which we again run away every time anything remotely challenges our irrational perceptions.

Our every move is controlled by a set of well-concocted lies as we trip over our Pinocchio noses, reacting as if trapped in an endless and repetitive script. It's a psychological Groundhog Day[3] where we repeat the same scenes with the same ending, never thinking to rewrite the script. We become our own self-fulfilling prophecies as subconscious fear produces more of the same things from which we are fooled into thinking we are protecting ourselves. Better said, deep down we expect more of the same, we act that way, and then when that harvest slaps us in the face, we holler, "*I told you so!*" never realizing our actions perpetuated the negative outcome.

Script Behavior

A script is a psychological term for how we react to the lying schemes (Fake-enlies) we set up in our subconscious. It takes no mental effort for this process. Each time we encounter an event, we jump into automatic script behavior. It's our default setting, and as far as we're concerned, it's nothing out of the ordinary. But, again, if these default responses are based on wrong thinking, they often result in unintended negative outcomes. That is the progression.

An event occurs, we start with the irrational schemes, and then the resulting emotions trigger what I call "script behavior." It happens without effort as we go through yet another round with "here we go again."

Irrational Emotional Discharges

Irrational emotional discharges (IED) can detonate as unexpectedly as the individual explosive devices that lurk in the minefields of war. IED refers to any behavior or response that is disproportionate to the situation at hand. These IEDs are born out of the unrealistic scripts we've build up over time. Because this ruins relationships or draws the wrong relationships into our lives, surrendering to IEDs can be a major destiny destroyer.

When we operate out of false scripts (built up from the past), it results in irrational emotions that distort our here-and-now perceptions. We fall prey to distorted perceptions that drive irrational emotions. Those emotions move us to actions or behaviors that, if irrationally grounded, lead to devastating outcomes. Just as on a battlefield, you won't see an IED until it explodes; these irrational emotional discharges lie in wait just below the surface. One false move or misstep leads to a full-blown detonation, and without doubt, the destruction ends up as your harvest.

After my second divorce, I had no desire to start dating again because I just couldn't stomach the thought of the phoniness I perceived as part of the dating scene. I was still licking my wounds and felt that one more lie was not going to result in a good outcome for the poor guy who chose to let it out of his mouth. It's not in me to put on airs to impress others, and I had no clue how to go about finding a man who could reciprocate that honesty. I figured God didn't need my help in the find-a-good-man department, and I was perfectly happy to just let it go.

Eventually I chose to start two long-distance relationships with a couple of gentlemen from my past. One was separated from his wife; the other was still married. Both were inaccessible from a commitment standpoint. I had known these gentlemen for years, so I knew what to expect. There was no chance of getting serious, and there was enough distance to allow me to feel safe. Eventually I began to feel guilty about pursuing the married man. I knew it was not God's desire for me to be committing adultery. It started to feel as if I was in a tug-of-war: Team Living-in-the-Past against Team Destiny. I knew God was somewhere in the Team-Destiny mix, but I wasn't in the mood to move on. I just kept pulling back hard and heavy on the rope, never looking to see who my teammates were.

As time progressed, I became very dissatisfied with both relationships. It was easy to let go of the guy who was separated from his wife. Letting go of the married man wasn't as easy because he had been a part of my life since 1980. But even that relationship got worrisome eventually — I was glad to see him coming but even gladder to see him going. The guy, I'll call him Bill, started to really get on my nerves when I noticed our conversations weren't much different from the past. He still talked about the same unfulfilled dreams he'd had decades ago, and he was always complaining about the same old relationship drama. He was still spewing pipedreams. I was on to new accomplishments.

As my dissatisfaction grew and God revealed the root of the fear behind my isolating, I started to make deliberate moves toward being more sociable. I intentionally forced myself to do little things I'd wanted to do for years. I started with a simple walk through East Grand Rapids. I even considered ballroom dance lessons. Okay, I never followed through on the dance lessons, but I did start attending social gatherings alone. One of those gatherings was a wedding reception for a family friend. The night before the wedding, I helped set up and found myself in a dialogue with my brother-in-law about my dream man. My cousin overheard the conversation and suggested I meet his friend, Marcus, who was planning to attend the gathering. Had I not vowed to do better socially, I would never have been open to this.

Marcus and I hit it off fantastically. He had a great sense of humor and was quick to pick up on mine. I was shocked at how easy the encounter was. That it could be so easy to slip back into the dating scene was unexpected because I had visions of multiple encounters with men with whom I couldn't be myself. I was myself that day without compromise, and the next thing we knew they were folding up the tables around us. I ended my thirty-year relationship with Bill.

Marcus and I got along very well for the first three months. It was my first relationship with a man who seemed to know the Bible inside out. We had numerous theological conversations. I mean, when the man said he had an Interlinear Bible, I thought I had someone who was on sound theological ground. He was the first man I had ever dated who initiated prayer with me. We prayed together almost every night and every morning. I thought he was the one.

Duped Again

Everything was great until I ran into financial challenges. I had put over three thousand dollars into my thirteen-year-old car just to keep it running. With the bankruptcy, I was on a tight budget that didn't allow for expensive repairs. It was time to seriously consider replacing the car, but a car payment wasn't in the picture. When Marcus learned about my dilemma, I sensed a shift in the relationship. Suddenly he had to go to Mississippi to visit his sick uncle for a month. When he returned he was too sick to answer the phone, and he didn't want me to see him like that. For two months afterward, he just couldn't find a way to come see me instead of my coming to see him.

The writing was on the wall. Stupid me, I was expecting the man to just come out and say he was no longer interested. He put himself out there as if he just says what's on his mind, *"whether you like it or not."* That didn't turn out to be the case. I found out that his "sick uncle" was a longtime girlfriend he's had since before his marriage ended. There was also a girlfriend in Pontiac, Michigan he failed to mention. This flew in the face of his unsolicited declarations of exclusivity in our relationship. I even had reason to believe he had added at least one other woman to the rotation. Wasn't that convenient: one in Grand Rapids, one in Mississippi, one in Pontiac, and another close to home? The most frightening thing about it was this man, in the face of confrontation and in the face of hard evidence, refused to admit his wrong. I got threats, avoidance, everything but an admission of the truth. Here we go again, another liar. When will it end?

In My Script

I was absolutely miserable and unable to function because I was replaying the same old lies I'd believed in the past. This mental scheme played out:

It was my fault for dating him. What's wrong with me? What is so innately wrong that I keep choosing the wrong men? Why do I keep falling for this same sorry scene over and over and over again? It's my fault he cheated on me. What evil inside draws this type of man to me repeatedly? I'm a bad person. I have a twisted psyche. It was entirely my fault. After eight years of prayer and soul searching, I'm still a hopeless case. I have to figure out what my problem is.

I was in my script, crying, depressed, and as usual internalizing this man's mistreatment as if it was my fault and I deserved it all because I believed the same old scheming lies.

Suddenly I remembered: Wait a doggone minute here. It was this knucklehead who pointed out not to internalize this stuff. I was guilty of nothing other than trusting him. It was freeing to see that the "bad" belonged to him for being such a lying cheat. This equal-opportunity scoundrel treated everybody that way. He was that way when we met, he was that way before we met, and he'll probably be that way from now on. I decided not to take it personally and moved on without a bit of shame or regret.

Keeping It Real

Thoughts and the behaviors they drive don't happen without an emotional catalyst. The scars and bruises we bear in our souls power our emotions. That's where we hold things we experience, good or bad. It's where we bear life's battle scars, healed or not. When we think we have dealt with something, but we haven't, the scars look healed but actually fester below the surface forming our frame of reference. One false move and those suckers pop wide open, and we're off and running as if the initial trauma is back in full force.

Meanwhile we keep taking on toxic relationships that support the rigid beliefs. If we fear rejection, we put on defenses to keep people at bay. We seek relationships with people who are emotionally unavailable, and when it doesn't work out, we see it as justification of our perspectives and expectations. If an opportunity for a healthy relationship comes along, we fail to recognize the blessing, or we ruin it because we're not emotionally healthy enough to maintain it. We create deep-seated expectations of more of the same trauma and hurtful experiences that keep us blind to truth.

Because our emotions are subconsciously driven, we're in full-blown script behavior whenever one of those festering wounds is touched off. The impact of the fallout far outweighs our initial intent as we leave residual devastation in our paths. It's counterproductive and self-defeating. Meanwhile we just move on, feeling we are the ones who have been mistreated or misunderstood, never realizing we are the problem. If we don't have some immovable standard to hold on to, we are incapable of recognizing what is real and what is not. No matter how highly degreed you are, no matter what your profession or ministry, this dynamic can take over. It did just that in the case of Marie and Gerard, two very intelligent and well-accomplished people.

Gerard is an expert in his field. Along with his Wall Street experience and an impressive and progressive work history, his certifications and background are unmatched. In his fifties, he commands a pretty penny. He could be a major asset to any team. Notice I said could be. To any onlooker Gerard is progressive, capable, extremely intelligent, and very handsome. But talk to the woman who loves him, and the backstory emerges.

Marie, also in her fifties, is twice divorced. She and Gerard met on a prominent online dating site. About six months into the relationship, they had an argument that was set off by a misunderstanding. She said, "blah-se-*splee*," he heard "blah-se-*whee*," and that's when it all started. She couldn't understand what was so bad that he was going to leave her. He refused to talk and made it clear he didn't want to hear anything she said. He was withdrawn and sulking, refusing to do anything other than to pout. Eventually he admitted he was off to the proverbial races on a train of thought based on something she never said. They got through it and moved on until the cycle repeated six months later.

Things came to a head after about a year into his unemployment. The arguments became more frequent as Gerard became more withdrawn and sullen. He became extremely judgmental and bossy. His moods swung like a pendulum from one day or minute to the next, and she found herself walking on eggshells trying to keep the peace. She finally asked him to leave.

The day she did so, she decided to unload all the things she had been stuffing away, and she got the best night's sleep in months. As a psychiatrist, she knew exactly where the problem was, and she was fed up with being afraid of the inevitable blowup because he didn't want to hear what she had to say. Based on my own professional expertise and my observations of this couple, she was quite accurate in fleshing things out.

As an adult child of two alcoholic parents, Gerard channeled his energies into proving his father wrong by making a name for himself in his chosen profession. It appears as if his father's negative reinforcement worked in his case. But in the here-and-now, the negative thoughts were pervasive and maladaptive, manifesting in an extremely defensive persona that, according to Marie, he couldn't overcome. He talked himself out of opportunities and ideas before even trying. Any outside suggestion or any guidance from her, no matter how right it might have been, was immediately met with why it wouldn't work. She described Gerard as highly opinionated and intolerant to opposing points of view.

Marie says she had overheard conversations between Gerard and many job recruiters in which his tone and attitude were as bad as with her. To no avail, she had repeatedly told him she did not appreciate his condescension and controlling behaviors. It didn't appear to matter to him at all that his tone was verbally abusive. She believed that was the reason he had been unemployed for so long.

With such a stellar background and international credentials, what else could be holding him back? He even said someone on one of his last jobs described him as "grouchy." He laughed it off, not realizing the people were saying exactly what she had been trying to tell him. The recruiters would invariably say at some point in the conversation, *"I'm sorry if I offended you"* or *"I didn't mean to offend you."* He was thinking he had been blackballed, and she was thinking he was right. But to this day, he still does not connect it with repeated warnings about his attitude and tone.

The Backstory

Gerard never talked much about his mother. He talked about his father sometimes, but all Marie got about his mother were bits and pieces here and there, after which came the unfailing, *"I'll have to tell you about it someday."*

Gerard has a form of Mosesitus — the same slave mentality that tethered the children of Israel to their prior bondage. He couldn't see the grapes, so to speak. As long as he refused to talk about whatever it was, he was stuck right where he was. Regardless, their relationship hung in the balance, and the final outcome hung on his willingness to change. That couldn't happen until he admitted he had a problem. He never did, so the relationship ended as suddenly as it had started.

Gerard is a prime example of how talent, skill, and ability can be locked down, immobilized by the grip of the past. Gerard was blind to his own personal responsibility because his defensive armor was so entrenched and his ego so fragile that every expression of love was suspect, and any constructive criticism or correction represented a personal affront.

It's not a stretch to see how attitude hinders personal and professional relationships. It sabotages teamwork in career settings and makes for a sorry leader because leaders must first know how to follow. In effect, Gerard's dad is still screaming in his ear, and he's dragging around the corpses of his parent's unresolved issues.

If We Can't Face It, God Can't Fix It

Look, if you've been through something you can't talk about its grip will only tighten. Fake-enstein has his hand over your soulish mouth because he knows that speaking out about the pain takes all the wind out of his sails. Until you turn around, face it, and unload that dead weight, you will never heal. In the profound words of Catherine Austin Fitts, "*If we can't face it, God can't fix it.*"[1]

One of my ex-husbands could never face his childhood trauma. I pieced together that he had been sexually traumatized as a child, but he couldn't face that horror. He said he couldn't remember anything about his recurring nightmares. He was running scared about something that ultimately landed him in prison for the rest of his life. At one point, he claimed to be in treatment. I later learned he had never darkened the door of a therapist.

Find somebody you can trust and unload what happened to you. Nine times out of ten, it wasn't your fault. Even if you did make mistakes in the past, they don't have to be your current reality. Letting it out deflates the big, bad monster you *think* lurks behind the closet door. It will run out squeaking like a mouse, and you'll wonder what took you so long.

It took me over thirty years to get to this truth because it took that long for me to tell someone about that rape thirty years prior. The day I did, I got free and was able to move forward in my purpose. Until then I was in the dark, face to face with that corpse, unable to see in front of me. I was completely unaware that I was operating under what I call a *total eclipse of the mind.*

Total Eclipse of the Mind

In itself, the human mind is unable to fathom the things of God. It's God's enemy. It's that key point of attack for enemy forces. As Joyce Meyer says, it's the battleground. As long as we don't understand this aspect of ourselves, we are doomed to dance as marionettes at the whim of the enemy. The consummate maestro, he orchestrates a circumstance here and an event there just to jerk our strings, and then he sits back with a bowl of popcorn to enjoy the performance. The whole time we're yelling, *"The devil is a lie!"* he's laughing and saying, *"And you believe quite a few of them, or you wouldn't be getting jerked around like this."* It's subtle and insidious. We don't even see how it poisons our very existence or how fear enslaves us on multiple levels. We are afraid, so we hole up in our own little worlds, wondering at the loneliness we, ourselves, perpetuate.

The Defense Dynamic

Defenses defeat their own purposes. They perpetuate the very things from which we are trying to protect ourselves. They are no more than strategic roadblocks to spiritual and emotional growth. They imprison us in a perpetual cycle of unintended consequences ranging from unhealthy relationships and stagnant career advancement, to health problems and general dysfunction in all areas of our lives. Unrecognized and unchecked, the cycle spins out of control while we sit deer-in-the-headlights stunned, in the consequential aftermath.

We can't possibly fathom how our perspectives have been clouded by our suffered pain and trauma. Rather than dealing with (and working through) painful experiences, we are caught up in a vicious cycle of poor choices that perpetuate, rather than alleviate, the problem. It's an extremely subtle progression. This relentless deterioration of our characters takes on the forms of denial, avoidance, blaming, guilt, shame, and other negative emotions. Instead of protecting us, they fuel smoldering fires that we ourselves can't see.

These defenses simply don't exist from our perspective. Yet everyone we meet is the unsuspecting recipient of the fallout perpetuated by who we *think* we are. We don't even know we're affected, or infected might be a better word. This poison isn't localized. It impinges on every aspect of our lives because we interpret life events through that filter. This undeniable roadblock to destiny doesn't go away without the determined effort that first begins with accepting that our own perceptions might be off — in some cases *way* off. With pain and trauma distorting the core aspect of our beings, we are effectively blocked from the spiritual and personal growth necessary to recognizing, realizing, and appreciating our purpose. We have to deliberately push past our defensives and replace knee- jerk Fake-enstein responses with behaviors grounded in purpose, destiny, and a focus on accomplishing our assigned missions in the Master Plan.

Defense and Denial: Siamese Twins

Defense and denial are Siamese twins that draw life from each other. They form conjoined forces though a system of beliefs intended to ward off any information that contradicts whatever entrenched irrational thoughts they fuel. Defense mechanisms, by their very nature, are as involuntary and unpredictable as the blink of an eye.

Denial cloaks reality by distorting, transforming, or otherwise falsifying how we see it. In this condition, we might as well be living some virtual existence in a parallel universe because our distorted perceptions don't line up with the reality at hand. Dealing with reality touches off feelings reminiscent of a negative, difficult, or even traumatic experience, and though that happened years or maybe decades ago, we'll do anything necessary not to go there again. So we don't let reality in.

The result of keeping reality at bay is subconscious anxiety, and then it is defenses to the rescue. The objective is to keep a comfortable enough level of denial to maintain equilibrium within the emotional pod we have created for ourselves. We're so stuck in denial we don't see that this shell of a pod is egg fragile, full of cracks and weak spots. But we go on fooling ourselves about it because we're in control of our pod. Nobody is in here but us chickens! We cower safely in this weak pod of fear unaware that our ostrich behinds are still flailing in the wind. While we're stuck in a time warp, with our heads buried in the sands of the hourglass, time and eternity march on, as life goes on around and without us.

WHOSE APPLE IS IT, ANYWAY!

The whole time I was in my abusive first marriage, it never crossed my mind to tell my parents the man was beating me up. It was so much of a non-option to me that it was nowhere in my thinking that it would be okay to tell them. In hindsight, that made no sense at all. I had heard the story about my father's confronting a man for putting his hands on one of my aunts. It's my understanding the domestic violence ended, and they are very happily married to this day. The rational consideration that he would do no less for his own daughter escaped me as I endured years of emotional and physical abuse. I was in a cloud quietly taking my lumps and denying that I deserved better or that I could do better. It would be years before I would ever tell my mother. I never discussed it with my father.

Not one of us is immune to this experience. It doesn't matter how much theological expertise you have, how many preaching skills you possess, or the size of your congregation. It doesn't matter how popular the ministry. It just doesn't matter. As long as we are bound in these bodies, we have to deal with these psychological and spiritual realities. We can continue ignoring our issues, or we can acknowledge them and submit to God's higher purpose by allowing Him to guide us through the healing process. Anything less dooms us to a repetitious past while destiny hangs in limbo.

Chapter 2: The Fruit of the Matter

Y ou cannot separate decision from destiny. They are dynamically and inextricably linked in the here and now. It's through free will and the power of choice that we determine our futures. Our daily decisions and behaviors either help or hinder our purpose, propelling us toward or away from destiny. Mosesitus (denial) has no regard for spiritual matters of purpose, calling, mission, and destiny, and it has no regard for God.

Fake-enstein (Defense System) rears his ugly head at every possible opportunity. If it happens at a spiritual crossroads, it's too bad for you. Strike up another one for the opponent and head to the sideline. You will surely have another opportunity to get it right. That's the rule. You may think you are making progress, but you have to learn the lesson before you can move forward on the Path of Purpose. Each step of it adds wisdom and guidance. It's a healing path of self-reflection and accountability. Each step, my friend, prepares you for the mission; it aligns you with destiny. In Israel's case, God couldn't penetrate their attitudes, and He can't penetrate ours. That's the first place we need to stop fooling our spiritual selves. In Mosesitus mode, Fake-enstein has us completely hijacked. We are asleep at the wheel while collateral damage perpetuates in our lives and the lives of those to whom we are connected. We move from one trauma to the next, sucking it up and fooling ourselves that we have dealt with it, while all we've really done is to stuff it down. We just cram it all into some imaginary internal boxes, shove them into our emotional closets, and slam the doors.

As long as nobody brushes up against that doorknob, we successfully compartmentalize blow after blow until it seeps into our character. It takes root burrowing, like tentacles, winding around, and choking out every aspect of our God-given personalities until even we are fooled into thinking it's who we really are. After a while, we react to situations, circumstances, and people based on Fake-enlies. We react in the present, not based on the current situation but on unresolved issues. Simply said, the entire mission is at stake, you can't effectively execute your calling, and your whole purpose for existing is on lockdown. Déjà vu, shades of the Garden of Eden, and shadows of the Exodus — by now we should get a clue. Enemy strategy hasn't changed one bit from the beginning. No different than Adam and Eve, Moses, or the nation of Israel, even in this new millennium here we stand... still duped.

The Big Picture

One night, as I talked with my mother and little sister, Susan, I said something that had to sound prideful. In the context of a discussion on destiny and greatness, I mentioned the opportunities and divine connections God had orchestrated in my life. Listing my abilities and talents, I said, *"God didn't give one person all that for no reason."* At that point, I understood my responsibility to allow God to use me as He desires. I had yet to learn it's not about how much talent and ability I have. It is about whether, through obedience and God's grace, those talents and abilities benefit others. Outside of that, none of it profits anybody, least of all me. So, once I had a higher focus, I had to get myself together so I wouldn't have to deal with God's showing me how my failure to get with the program caused Him to have to find somebody else to do what He had assigned to me. He's not going to be hearing excuses; there are none. As He once told me, I know better. After all, destiny is not a given; it comes at a price.

I'm reminded of something my mother told me in one of my darkest hours. It was mid-afternoon and I was still in bed with all the blinds closed, worn out by yet another blow to the heart in a rope-a-dope marriage and grappling with the depression that all but took me out for good. I mustered the strength to pick up the phone, and she proceeded to drop the mother lode of wake-up wisdom.

"Linda, I don't think there are two people from the beginning of time until Jesus comes who have gone through what you've been through. This isn't about you. It's about all the people who will be set free as a result of what you're going through." She went on to say that I was going to write a book and go on the conference circuit. I didn't want to hear any of it at the time. But in the middle of being irritated, I knew Mom was speaking into my life.

It had happened before when she said I was going to move back to Michigan. I didn't want to hear that either. One month later, I'd sold everything, left Chicago after eleven years, and here I sit today in Grand Rapids, Michigan, where I have been for over twenty years. So when she told me I was going to write a book, as outlandish as that sounded, I knew she was again speaking into my life.

Interrelationship

We're all universally and inextricably connected because God has chosen to accomplish His will on earth through us. We only fool ourselves to think anything we do occurs in a vacuum or by a team of one, so relationships are very important. There are few people in life I dislike at first sight, and I don't nurture dissention or stay in contentious relationships. Yet there have been a few times when I would meet someone and immediately things take a combative tone.

The old Linda used to engage that negativity. I've learned since that more times than not these are divine connections written into the Master Plan. Without fail, these people have become very dear to me and played significant roles in my personal, professional, and spiritual growth. We need each other. God orchestrates our destinies through other people. If one of us is out of commission, it affects some other part of the Master Plan.

The defense mechanisms we take on to protect ourselves become rigid, fear-driven systems of thought that keep us reacting to events long passed — something none of us can change. When we act out of that fear, reacting over and over again to the same past traumatic event, we destroy relationships and block avenues to destiny. It stunts spiritual growth and creates a roadblock to recognizing that we are the problems we seek to rectify. Meanwhile others have no clue about what our problem is. They react out of their defenses, and it's an endless, useless cycle of doing everything but cutting to the heart of the matter. Nobody is operating out of their True Selves, and nobody's seeing anything but the other person's Fake-enstein.

This is not good in professional or personal relationships. But Old Fakey is relentless, and every contention we nurture, every internalized wrong that causes us to lash out is another nonrealistic reaction designed to destroy the very relationships God orchestrated to facilitate our purpose. We have to recalibrate our focus to overcome this trap. We have to stop thinking about our own protection long enough to see past someone else's.

Mama saw the big picture while I was wallowing in tears of anger, frustration, bitterness, and at one point, thoughts of suicide. I was in a moment-by-moment battle for survival. I was in spiritual boot camp. It was one of many do-or-die moments. After getting over being angry at the messenger, I moved on to her message and decided to refocus. That decision served me well, because at that point I had more work to do one on one with God. He was not letting me walk out of that marriage unless and until I worked through decades of issues I had stuffed away, the whole time thinking I had addressed them. He knew that to let me out of that hell before I had worked through it, would find me back where I started in denial, stunted spiritual growth, and incapacitated for duty.

It's Not about You

To effectively leverage our God-given ability to choose, we have to first grasp this truth: It's not about us. It's about the Master Plan, the big picture, the overall goal. This is a difficult concept when it's your tail in the fire, but it's a whole lot easier to act right when you have that higher focus. That focus is important because the intricacies of our intertwined lives are unfathomable. We may never know the number of people we influence or with whom our destinies are intertwined. I've had people from high school tell me how something I did or said influenced their lives. Like them, I was just feeling my teenage way through life. I wasn't focused on impressing anyone. I remember a particular young lady who expressed how it changed her relationship with God to see me perform during a church service. I was deeply touched. All I was doing was what I loved — music. In the meantime, somebody was so blessed they never forgot it.

Got a Lot of Nerve

As I drove to work one day, this concept struck home. At the time, I was barely treading the waters of depression and sorting through the emotional and financial fallout of divorce. I was on my way to homelessness and bankruptcy. Looking around, there was nobody in a position to help. I realized I had a lot of counterproductive relationships that were more of a drain than edifying on any level. I decided to cut everybody loose, including that ex-husband who found every opportunity to drop by my job for a chat. I was an emotional basket case, but I felt pretty good about my decision. On some level, I even felt superior to those jokers.

As I was driving along half listening to the radio, half zoning out, I suddenly saw myself sitting in a pile of ashes, covered in dust. I was gray head to toe with a hill-shaped pile of dust on top of my head: Job! Then I saw two of the folks I had just cut loose sitting on either side of me. They were gray too. But I was the only one with a pile on my head. Though it wasn't outwardly audible, I heard the Lord say, *and you're one of 'em!* Catching that revelation, I wiped the stupid look off my face and laughed aloud, *"Lord, that'll preach!"* But He wasn't through! He said . . . *and you're the worst of all of them because you know better.*

Wow! What a colossal slap in the face. There I was teetering between indignation at being wronged and realizing it was all due to my own sorry choices. It never occurred to me that I was no better than they were, let alone worse. How do I get off feeling superior to anybody? I was all puffed up because I finally wanted better for myself compared to what I judged as their unenlightened conditions. I thought, Don't I have some nerve! Here I am standing at the corner of Stuck-on-Stupid Street and Better-do-Better Boulevard, and I can't even take the bus because I've got a purse full of nothing but consequences. How do I dare feel superior to anybody?

I remembered how for years my mother had been praying and believing for a new house. What if I'm what's holding up that blessing? And if I am, how many others are waiting for blessings God wants to channel through me? Well, that's all it took to knock me off my high horse. That new revelation shifted my focus to higher spiritual ground as I caught the true vision of purpose. Our focus shouldn't be fulfilling our purpose as a route to our own happiness. Of course, that's an inevitable by-product of it, but it should never be the main focus. Our channeling blessings and kingdom resources to others is the goal. Facilitating purpose (ours or others') with a focus on destiny ensures we aren't jamming up the intricate workings of the Master Plan.

Chapter 3: Whose Apple is it, Anyway!

Looking back to the Garden of Eden, the Bible doesn't specify that the fruit Adam and Eve ate was an apple, but for purposes of this discussion, let's just call it one. So whose apple was it anyway? At the end of the ensuing blame game, was that question ever answered?

Adam's blaming Eve didn't fly. In his case, it wasn't about Eve. What was at issue was his reaction to her disobedience. Eve's declaration of being duped by the snake didn't hold water either, but to her credit, she did have enough sense not to blame Adam. Poor Adam, not only does he take the rap for the whole human condition, but that dad-gum apple's been his ever since. The truth is, it wasn't at all about Eve, and it was never Adam's apple. It wasn't about the apple at all. The apple wasn't at fault for the Fall of Man. Man was.

Adam and Eve, in the face of God's orders to the contrary, ate the fruit. It could have been a turnip; it doesn't matter. What matters are Adam's and Eve's choices. The apple merely marked the crossroads of destiny or destruction. At their crossroads, Adam and Eve took the wrong path and reaped a commensurate harvest. In the face of temptation their decisions didn't align with God's Creative Purpose and wound up short-circuiting the very destiny they lived.

The fruit from the Tree of the Knowledge of Good and Evil was "pleasing to the eye and good for food" (Genesis 2:9). The fruit itself was perfectly fine except for this: they were told not to eat it. So why did God put it there in the first place and then tell them not to eat from it? I mean, perfect garden, Tree of Life. What was the point?

Without *both* trees, there was no choice. He wanted us to exercise the free will He gave us, even though it could have, and has indeed, mucked up the mechanisms of the Master Plan. That's how important free will is to God. Adam and Eve could have easily eaten from the Tree of Life. Even though both trees were located at the center of the garden, they never chose to eat *that* fruit (see Genesis 3:22). Instead, Adam and Eve stood smack-dab mid-destiny and chose to "do the goofy." They didn't do it in some far-off land dreaming of a yet-to-be-realized, age-old promise. They were hewn from the very destiny they walked. They knew nothing but God's Creative Purpose. They lived it, and with that decision, they *left* it. Still, we're left with that doggone apple.

What's with that Apple?

The apple represents situations and circumstances we encounter. It can be any life challenge. It can be the coworker who tap dances on your last nerve or the person who knows how to push your buttons in the right order. It can be a habit you want to break. It could be a wrong you unjustly suffered, an insult, a barb here, or a misunderstanding there. It can be that recurring emotional outburst after which you feel defeated because you were determined not to let it happen again.

The apple could be anything that keeps recurring in your life the reasons for which you're clueless. It can be people, places, circumstances, or events — anything that sets off your defensive triggers and blinds you to truth, thus diverting focus from the core matter. It's not the situations, circumstances, people, or other things at issue, as much as it is what you do or don't do in the face of them. It's at the core that we find the cure. However, when we're in Mosesitus (denial) mode, we're usually blind to core issues.

What Eve Missed

The serpent's underlying motivation was revenge. For him it wasn't at all about Eve, although that's what he led her to think. At the core (where the seed resides), he had a major axe to grind with God. His entire focus was retaliation for his own rebellious hinny getting booted out of heaven. Eve failed to recognize the seed of that apple. If she had, she would have figured out she did not have to ascribe to somebody else's retaliatory rebellion. Playing right into his hands, she ingested that fruit, summarily internalizing the serpent's rebellion. She gave up ground to the enemy, right along with her God-conferred dominion. She traded her harvest for his and wound up suffering a similar fate — kicked out of Eden. She should not have taken that apple, and neither should you!

It's the same old Garden Game — the same old scene with different players, same director. Meanwhile, nobody has a clue about the backstory or should I say the back-*corey* (what's at the core of a matter). There isn't enough written about Eve's personality to decipher the specifics of her issues. Because she was human, though, we can safely assume the serpent was playing on a weakness he identified in her character. Eve might have seen through to the core of the matter had she not been blinded by whatever character issue the serpent played on.

What issues could she have had? She had no childhood to be mucked up, and it was only God, Adam, and her in the garden. What kind of life experiences could have mutated her character? Probably nothing, but that's an ongoing theological debate. Whatever it was is tied to her humanity, something with which we all grapple. In the overall scheme of things, it doesn't matter now that the deal is done. But here's the kicker: if Eve was prone to this human condition without being twisted up by life, how much more are we Fake-enstein prone (denial prone) folks subject to this blindness? We can't see the core of the apples we're accepting, let alone their phony seeds.

Phony Apple Seeds

The apple is made up of the peel, flesh, core, seeds, stem, and leaves. But the seeds deceive. As delicious as it was, you could plant that apple's seed, thoroughly expecting the same juicy, tasty apple. But what you'll get is some mutation of that apple, completely unrecognizable and sometimes tasteless.1 No aspect of it will be the same. That's because an apple grows from a pollinated blossom. Who knows how many other types of blossom dust got caught up in the mix?

The little bumblebee happily flits from tree to tree while contaminating the whole gene pool! These hybrid seeds are very difficult to geminate. They take a lot of extra time and care to grow. So germinating bogus seed is a waste of precious time spent cultivating somebody else's less-than-stellar harvest.

The fruit you get might not even tolerate your climate. After years of germinating and cultivating, the fruit rots on the branch or the tree dies before the fruit ever matures. If it pays off at all, you might get an apple, but it's what's at the core that counts. The seeds will never produce another apple exactly like it, because it can only reproduce the conglomerate of DNA that pollinated it. Great! Now you have taken on somebody else's seed, and it is a bad fit. You are out of balance as you try to make it yours. Again precious time and energy is diverted from purpose and destiny. What went wrong?

The apple blossom will produce more of the same delicious fruit as long as its branch is grafted into the right tree. In that case, it does not matter how many different types of pollen get into the mix; the tree consistently produces the same type of apple. If we are to recognize and root out the seeds of the past, we have to be grafted into the higher thoughts of God, holding that as the unchanging standard of truth. Just as apple tree branches have to be grafted into the root of a tree to produce more apples of its kind, we have to be rooted into something higher, truer, eternal, and unchanging.

If the seed that has taken root does not line up with God's Word or His direct instruction to you, it has to go — no questions asked, no mulling it over, no wallowing in it. It's a seed that belongs in the distant past. It's seed thrown from somebody else's harvest. But because we have been operating in Fake-enstein mode so long, we have to train ourselves to see the core of it and recognize the motives seeding our own defenses before we can even begin to discern seeds that belong to others.

The APPLE Inventory

To leverage painful experiences we have to recognize bogus fruit grown from counterfeit seed and weed it out. One bad apple left unchecked will rot anything it touches. Too many rotten apples make it almost impossible to decipher which one started the deterioration. It takes skill not to keep adulterating our future harvests by internalizing bogus seeds and perpetuating the same bad crop of fruit.

How we behave is at the crux of the harvest matter. We just keep catching those bad apples and taking them into our harvest. We wrongly keep throwing bad seed after bad seed. It's the perpetual Eve Syndrome where we blindly take that fruit as offered, because it keeps Fake-enstein comfortable. Fake-enstein keeps us open to enemy attack through weaknesses in our characters developed from enduring and internalizing the wrongs of others. Once this entry is shut off, we are in control of the war, and we will lose fewer and fewer battles along the way. Remember the Exodus. The battles are inevitable, but the losses are unnecessary; that is, with the proper strategy.

Here and Now

We plant our harvest in the here and now. Farmers who sit back waiting for a harvest before they plant seeds, get zilch in return. Yet that is what many of us do. We are in church naming, claiming, declaring, believing, and wondering why it's taking so long. We're yelling at the devil, calling him a lie, never realizing we're living the very lies he's telling. We're praying for a better harvest, the whole time planting and cultivating bogus seeds. We're throwing bad after bad just because some other deluded Fake-enstein threw apples at us, and we reciprocated in kind.

We have to plant in the present. We sow our harvests by how we act right now. Yes, that means even in the middle of adversity and wrong, in good times and bad. How we act is planting our own future harvests. What kind they are, again, is up to us. Are you seeding toward better crops or more of the same? Are you building toward mission and purpose, or are you building up more of what you've been getting in the past? If you are happy with the status quo, then all is well. But if there are any areas you know of that still need attention, it might behoove you to execute a bit of crop rotation. We don't want to plant our new crops among the bad.

Crop Rotation

In the interest of rotating out bad crop, we have to master skillful self- examination to weed out the bogusly seeded apples that are choking out our harvests. We begin where we have control — ourselves.

Without deseeding our own thoughts, we can't see clearly enough to recognize others' bad fruit before they get into our orchards. We initiate personal assessment using the APPLE Inventory to get a clear picture of our own fruit (rotten or not) and to identify where our issues bleed into those of others or trigger and/or encourage others' encroachment on our spiritual ground.

The following five-point evaluation flips the script on Irrational Emotional Discharges (IED) and Fake-enstein entrenchments that have been choking out our harvests. It exposes the thought patterns holding us back, stunting our spiritual growth, and thus setting up stagnation in all areas of our lives. By using the APPLE Inventory, we can root out the self-defeating and counterproductive thinking that block out purpose and short-circuit our destinies.

Let's examine our APPLE. These five areas require close examination to reveal blind spots in our characters. This powerful tool guides us through a truthful examination of self in order to root out where IEDs are hidden in various mindfields. The five areas that need examining are these:

- Attitude
- Perception
- Perspective
- Lies
- Expectations

These nuances are concrete in their existence, yet stealthy in their detection. We don't see ourselves clearly, so it takes a determined effort to root out their clandestine influences. We will start with attitude because it is the culmination of all the others.

Attitude

Almighty attitude rules! We cannot have enough talent, skills, or abilities to overcome a bad attitude. It propels us toward destiny or mires us in the past. Attitude reflects to others what we believe about the world around us and ourselves. Attitude is defined as "a position or manner of carrying oneself. Posture, a state of mind or a feeling. Disposition."[1]

The aeronautical application better highlights attitude's influence on purposeful focus and direction: "position of aircraft or spacecraft relative to a frame of reference (the horizon or direction of motion)."[2] So, the attitude of the plane is determined by how it is lined up with the horizon. Depending on pilot perception, the outcome could be crash and burn or a successful landing. If it is crash and burn, you can't blame the horizon because the earth is not moving to accommodate pilot error. Neither are reality and truth going to change to accommodate us.

Attitude is perfectly captured by Charles Swindoll's assessment of its importance to cultivating our harvests. He presents a comprehensive picture of its importance:

> *The longer I live, the more I realize the impact of attitude on life. Attitude, to me, is more important than facts. It is more important than the past, than education, than money, than circumstances, than failures, than successes, than what other people think or say or do.*[3]

All the things Swindoll listed are like the apple, not at fault and outside of your control.

> *It is more important than appearance, giftedness, or skill. It will make or break a company . . . a church . . . a home.*[4]

A bad attitude will always overshadow knowledge, skills, talents, and abilities because none of them matter outside of relationship. A bad attitude is a problem because it is through relationship that God accomplishes the Master Plan. We do not achieve purpose in a chasm, and we do not accomplish the mission without other people. Swindoll goes on to say,

> *The remarkable thing is we have a choice every day regarding the attitude we will embrace for that day.*[5]

And therein lays the power — the power to choose a better outcome. The power that resides in our God-given ability to choose.

> *We cannot change the inevitable. The only thing we can do is play on the one string we have, and that is our attitude.*[6]

Circumstances and situations come and go. How steady we are in the storm is a decision that's leveraged on the Path of Purpose, nowhere else. We can lead our lives being jerked around at the whim of circumstance, or we can ground ourselves in the truth of who we really are and then leverage the past in realizing our purposeful mission in the Master Plan.

> *I am convinced that life is 10 percent what happens to me, and 90 percent how I react to it. And so it is with you . . . we are in charge of our attitudes.*[7]

Our attitudes are propelling us a hundred miles an hour down life's runway. The plane is nosed toward or away from destiny. If we don't recalibrate our emotional instruments, we will wind up staring down the end of our lives, a payload of unfinished business in tow, all because we did not know that all it took was a shift in focus to alter our direction. Here's my University of Hard Knocks lesson: *Attitude Determines Altitude!* One day I was watching a man preach on 2 Chronicles from a perspective that had nothing to do with my own situation at work. It was early in my process of healing, and I was struggling with taking formal action against my supervisor. God had other plans in that regard. As I listened to the sermon, 2 Chronicles 20:17 hit me right between the eyes:

"Ye shall not need to fight in this battle: set yourselves, stand ye still, and see the salvation of the Lord with you, O Judah and Jerusalem: fear not, nor be dismayed, tomorrow go out against them: for the Lord will be with you" (KJV).

What was that? How many times had I heard that account of Jehoshaphat and the Ammonites? This time, though, it had new significance: *"You will not file another grievance."* Okay, I recognize that voice! I knew God meant business. Even though more than one person described my supervisor's treatment as discriminatory, the Lord flat refused to allow me to file any other grievance or complaint.

Stand still and see His salvation. In other words, Linda, you are done fighting these battles and defending yourself. Whatever happens, you'll work as if you're working for Me, period. What that entailed became more painfully evident with each time I had to shut my mouth although everything raging inside was screaming, "Speak up!" Every time I had to humble myself under my supervisor's authority, even when she was treating me wrongly, there I was seething and biting my tongue.

At first it took all I could muster, because I had to fight through deep-seated rage, but over time I went from "stand still and see" (all the wrong treatment) to "stand still and watch" (humbling myself and subjugating my feelings to God as He moved on my behalf). Watch. Yeah, right. I wish all it *took* were watching. I don't know why the Lord gave me such a love for this woman — it only made it hurt more when she mistreated me. One day He said, "She is not the problem. There are things inside you that I want to work out." Her being as wrong as two left shoes was not the issue. In the overall scheme of things, it was what was going on inside *me* that mattered.

That would be my first lesson in *"What did I tell you to do?"* Circumstances and mistreatment by others do not constitute loopholes or fine print in the contract. Whatever He tells me to do is what I am held accountable for, no matter what circumstances might appear to dictate. It took a few months of sucking it up before I realized *I* was a *walking piece-of- work* with a hellacious attitude. The Lord took a scalpel to that mess, and it didn't feel good at all!

One particularly frustrating day I remember saying, "*Lord, just let me learn whatever it is I need to learn so I can get out of here.*" I wanted out, but I knew I had to learn the lesson first. One gut-wrenching episode after another I had to stand in the face of opposition and keep my mouth shut. I suffered in miserable silence as my emotions rushed in at gale force. I had to stop it at the door.

I could not let it out of my mouth. For someone who has to get it said or get no rest, it was a notable accomplishment. It didn't happen overnight. I had multiple opportunities to develop my spiritual muscles along the way.

I knew by that time it was up to me to determine how long I stayed in what I perceived as dire straits. I was completely in control of whether I accepted the lesson I was to learn. As I moved into my True Self, I became free of that opinionated, angry, mess of a woman I used to be. A change of attitude also changed the way others related to me. My boss and I eventually became good friends, and to this day, over twenty years later, we still keep in touch.

We are our own worst enemies or our greatest allies when it comes to destiny. Without a routine personal inventory, we never know where we're open to enemy attack. We need to close those avenues by identifying blind spots and using them as opportunities for personal and spiritual development. As we move through personal inventory, we gain a new outlook on ourselves that expands or changes our frames of reference.

Perception (Lenses on the World)

Our perceptions are what feed our perspectives. They are as sunglasses that turn everything we see a shade of orange, yellow or green. The tint of the lenses determines how we see the world around us. If either lens is dirty, both the image and the colors are distorted. But, the glasses don't change the reality they distort. The trees are still the same shade of green God made them. The sky and water are the same shades of blue. Take off the glasses and you will see a more realistic world, and therein lays the rub. We don't see that we're wearing them, let alone know to take them off. We are in denial and can't see it any other way.

Self-Perception. The tinted glasses also distort our views of ourselves. Self- perception includes self-esteem (how well we think of ourselves) and self-efficacy (how capable we think we are). It is a clever point of attack indeed. If you can be convinced you can't do anything that is calling, purpose, and mission oriented, you won't do it.

This dynamic was in play when the Israelites' search party had differing opinions of what they had seen. Against all evidence to the contrary, the group who saw themselves as grasshoppers in the eyes of the giants did not believe they could take the land. Those siding with Joshua and Caleb believed they could do it. The outcome: they were both right. The group who died in the desert got what they perceived, and the believers who sided with Joshua and Caleb did too. One group never saw the promise, but the other group did.

Self-concept is the sum total of our beliefs and thoughts about ourselves, both individually and in relation to others. We perceive the actions of others based on how we perceive ourselves. This gets back to the Frame of Reference. If we have a very negative self-concept, no matter how good others are to us, we perceive their actions negatively. Of all the conclusions we draw from our experiences, self-perception is the driving force behind the attitude and personalities we present as who we are. This complicates clear communication and causes a huge gap between perceived intentions and reality. As a result, our abilities and talents are locked down. Even though we might have considerable accomplishments, the way we see ourselves in relation to others either draws the wrong people or relationships into our lives or hinders our progress on other levels. That knife cuts both ways.

Man in the Mirror. To his credit, my second husband was highly intelligent, bordering on genius. His charisma and smile were unmatched. He could sing with so much power he would put down the microphone and his voice would still fill a noisy club. Oh, he was quite the charmer, master's degree and all. Time eventually revealed, though, that something was off.

In his subconscious lurked a secret so horrible he could never bring himself to get help. Too many nights I was awakened by blood-curdling screams unlike any horror movie sound effect. He insisted he could not remember what these dreams were about, even in their immediate aftermath. I pieced together that he had been sexually abused as a child. He told me of one incident after which he was rushed to the hospital bleeding.

Even knowing of his difficult upbringing, all I saw was the good that seldom came to the fore. I overlooked what life had twisted into a completely dysfunctional chameleon of a man with a please-me agenda that kept him, at the drop of a hat, transforming into whomever he thought the situation dictated. He had so many secrets he couldn't keep up. Encouraging and supporting his talents, skills, and abilities was like trying to push a rope. Everything I did just felt like an oppressive cloud hovering over the effort. I don't know if it was his lack of motivation or the spiritual heaviness that followed him around, but nothing ever worked.

We can only be as honest with others as we are with ourselves, so I remained completely deluded for years by lie after lie. His being like that was his responsibility to change. The fact that I chose to accept it was my bad. That it took so long for me to come to my senses is testament to my own self-concept, which made it easier to overlook reality than to face my fear of confrontation. I turned a blind eye, although my instincts were screaming, "*Wake up!*"

To the exclusion of all else, I focused on the person God created in him — a person he had never seen in himself. In the end it didn't matter what I saw when I looked at him. It was what *he* saw when *he* looked in the mirror that mattered in *his* life. In that case, the negative self-concept cut both ways. That is the usual dynamic. We attract the negativity we foster in our hearts. With me in Mosesitus mode, I was completely hijacked by Fake-enstein, and so was he. Our marriage was the perfect Fake-en*lie*! Now that I think about it, I was walking around internalizing rape (more than one, by the way. But that's one for the memoirs), so I got exactly that, a rapist. How's that for a wakeup call? The perfect example of how this works.

It's not necessarily that sick people are all deliberately on the prowl for prey. It's that their Fake-enstein is so strong they don't realize why they're attracted to weaker people, people who they can easily manipulate to keep from riling up Old Fakey! The manipulated are cluelessly going along because they are caught up in the lies they believe. When the lies can coexist without waking Old Fakey, what results is an unholy symbiotic mess.

Total Eclipse of the Blind. A few years ago, I struck up a relationship with Sandra, a single mother of two. Sandra is highly intelligent with butterscotch skin and a walk that exudes self-confidence. She turned heads when she walked into a room. Her presence was eclipsed only by her smile. I understood Sandra. I had a lot more patience with her than any other friend I have ever had. So, when her drinking brought out the controlling, demanding, and judgmental attitudes that put other people off, I loved her through it.

I could always see beyond the fallout and façade to a little girl cowering in the corner of her soul, vainly hiding from remnants of childhood sexual abuse, pent-up anger, fear, frustration, and bitterness. They had become constant companions, hovering shadows that never disappeared, not even in the light. Lurking in those shadows was a storm that rained incessant darkness over her entire life. The difference was that an eclipse passes over. A shadow you can ignore. This thing permeated her soul to the point of stifling any sense of self-esteem or self-efficacy that dared rear up, and no amount of encouragement made any difference. It had no practical power in her life.

I've now watched this young woman ravaged by prescription drugs and alcohol. She never keeps a job. She gets hired, likely because employers see her potential. She works long enough to claim unemployment. When it runs out, she looks for another job.

A negative self-concept and the enemy can sit back and relax because the whole kit and caboodle is a wash. Everybody in the universe can see you differently, but it doesn't matter if *you* don't get it. It's all about denial, my friend. It's all about blinded eyes denying truth, even if it's slapping us in the face, because we are ruled by our self-perceptions. As long as *they're* off, we're off destiny's track because we are not seeing the playing field the same way truth sees it. We are coming in for a landing at the wrong angle and expecting the terrain to change to accommodate it. Result? Crash and burn!

Emergent-See. One morning I woke up to what sounded like the smoke alarm. The air was smoky. Starting with the basement, I immediately sought the source. I checked the storage and laundry rooms, but not even those alarms were triggered. Moving to the living room, I noted the sound was louder, but the alarm was not triggered. I checked the bedroom, then went outside to check if I was seeing smoke from another fire. The smoke seemed as thick outside as inside.

Noticing a lady two doors down, I asked if she saw the smoke in the air. With a very strange look, she denied seeing any smoke. I walked around. Not believing she couldn't see it, I asked again, which elicited the same response. Irritated I went back in the house, got my cat, threw him the backseat of my car, and called the fire department.

Several firemen searched all three floors of the house, but they didn't see the smoke either. They checked all alarms to find them operable but discovered a malfunctioning carbon monoxide detector in the living room. After they left, I was still wondering why nobody else could see this smoke. By then I was convinced I could smell it too. So I was walking around, talking aloud about not understanding why nobody else could see this smoke. After all, it was even outside.

Eventually I rubbed my eyes and discovered I had slept in some cheap contact lenses I had bought at the beauty supply store. They always cloud up if I leave them in overnight. Once I removed them my vision began to clear up, and I realized I must have looked *fourteen-carat crazy*, eyes big as saucers, talking about nonexistent smoke. I was irritated with folks who were seeing clearly. But in my own eyes, smoke was infiltrating the *world*.

Until I rubbed my eyes, you could not have convinced me I was wrong. What a boss knucklehead! I would have given my life standing on my own truth that the house and the whole outdoors were full of smoke. When I finally woke up and joined the rest of civilization, I felt like an even bigger nut case than I must have appeared. Okay, while you're laughing, two words: *you too*!

That story demonstrates so well the phenomena I call Stuck on Stupid. That's how blind we are to our own messes. We see everybody else's problem, but not our own. You can imagine how strange I must have looked to everybody from the firemen to the neighbors. Think about how we look to others when we are entrenched in our own unrealistic perceptions. The way our characters get twisted from all the things we go through is played out in how we live and how we relate to others, but we can't see it. Denial is a dangerous state of mind because, generally, everybody but you sees there is something wrong. Yet *nobody* but you can change it.

Perspective

The sum total of all the conclusions we draw from our perceptions, *perspective is* the driving force behind the attitude and the personality we present to the world. Our perspective is based on our beliefs. It is our take on the world. Perspective can facilitate or hinder focus. A well-placed attack on perspective redirects vision. Vision is key to achieving purpose and destiny. It helps us in navigating the enemy's mindfields.

Perspective is negatively affected by residual damage from inflicted emotional wounds. We subconsciously set up a system of defenses, the goal of which is its own survival at all costs. Its weapon of choice is denial as it cloaks itself as an invisible force field against all realities it perceives as threats to its existence. The children of Israel were so severely affected by denial they perceived the very promise of God as a threat. Don't believe the emotional hype. Once Fake-einstein is in full effect, the lies go flying like arrows. The lies fuel the thoughts that chain us to the past like that Body of Death. It's dead weight.

Lies

What lies are you telling yourself? The lies we run without realizing it are like living by a railroad track. After a while, we tune out the sound of the trains. It's different with the trail of lies that drive our thoughts. Tune them out or not, they still wreak havoc in our lives.

I caught myself in this. Every time my guy and I had a falling out, I would start looking at all the things I thought were wrong with me. Maybe if I do this differently, I shouldn't do this, don't do that. It was always my own fault, never any of his responsibility. The minute I got wind that, I was doing that, I ended it right then and there. The peace that came behind that change held steady through every other disagreement. If any part was my bad, I apologized and moved on. If not, I just moved on. No nagging and nitpicking. I just moved on. I had already trained myself by going through the APPLE Inventory, owning up to my own part and making amends where necessary. After doing that we can take the lesson learned and leverage it going forward by not making the same mistake again.

To root out these lies, just take note of the things you tell yourself every day. Especially take note when you are upset about something. Deliberately pay attention to what you are saying to yourself. You might have to seek the help of trusted others who are not afraid to tell you the truth. Trust me. If you're telling yourself these lies, you have spilled the beans in conversations with others. But beware! What they say might sound completely foreign to you. Listen anyway. Take note. Take *notes* if you have to.

Expectations

Our expectations, whether expressed or not, conscious or subconscious, realistic or unrealistic, are born of our internal beliefs. In Fake-enstein mode, we are encumbered by past wrongs. Fake-einstein's whole existence is testament to the fact that we are expecting more of the same treatment. We would not need to protect ourselves if we were not expecting more wrong.

Fake-enstein feeds on Fake-enlies that weave the chain of thoughts that tie us to the past. Expectations, conscious or not, are reflected in our attitudes, perspectives, and perceptions. When fear-based they draw more negativity. Whether based on fear-fed Fake-enlies or in truth, expectations draw into our harvests more of their kind. It's no secret, no mystery. Fear breeds more fear, and every negative thought it spawns drives us is in a direction opposite our destiny.

That is where "reap what you sow" (Law of Attraction) is either friend or foe. You will draw whatever you are expecting. Expecting is a part of having faith, which is our belief in a given end result or outcome. When Fake-einstein goes rogue, fear overshadows faith, and the whole reap-what- you-sow thing still works but in an opposite direction. Instead of producing a destiny-inspired outcome, it can lead to self-defeat.

Expectations are self-fulfilling[9] prophecies whether they originate from fear or hope, good or bad. They result in purpose or defeat, destruction or destiny. This puts a whole new twist on "perception is reality." We think that applies when other people's perceptions are off and their delusions encroach on our realities. The truth is our own attitudes, perceptions, perspectives, lies, and self-concepts all come together to create the harvests we're standing in now. We're living our harvests. Our lives are evidence of our expectations. Whether they are on track with destiny and purpose is up to us.

It behooves us to do some serious checking into our expectations because Old Fakey and his IEDs are not having anything do with our destiny, and he couldn't care less about what that means for us. He knows, better than we do, that he is not part of the Master Plan. So he is fighting like crazy for his own existence. It's our thoughts driving the expectations that are keeping him alive.

Not sure where to start? Here's a clue: Look around you. Where do you stand in your life? Have you had multiple broken relationships? Are you experiencing career stagnation? Broke? Not seeing an end to the drama? Make a list and make a plan. It's time to recalibrate those expectations.

Consider this your take-stock inventory; your self-examination list, your reality check. Its purpose is to uncover areas in which your perspective might be off, leading to a distorted perception of current situations, circumstances, people, places or things that set you off. It will

guide you in uprooting the lies that drive unrealistic emotional responses to life events and shed light on the subconscious thoughts that are at the core of self-defeating and destiny-destroying beliefs that are negatively affecting your future harvest. Each time you get sidelined by an IED, take a step back and ask yourself:
1. Do I need an attitude adjustment? Is my attitude perpetuating negativity in this situation? How can I leverage my will to make a better choice as opposed to engaging negativity?
2. How do I position myself to look at the event from another perspective? Is my perspective correct or am I misperceiving the event.
3. Are my perceptions off? Am I reacting based on the facts of the situation or have I subconsciously read something from my past into the current event?
4. What irrational beliefs are at play in the current situation? What lies am I telling myself or believing? What is the truth of the matter?
5. What conscious or subconscious expectations are driving my reactions to the event?

Attitude, perspective, perceptions, lies and expectations (APPLE) bear the seeds that will plant a better harvest than you are standing in right now or perpetuating more of the same mess. Remember, it is the decisions you make, in the moment, that determine whether you're walking out the current mess into some more mess; or walking out of this mess into a better harvest.

What's Your *Apple*tude?

As we uncover who we really are, we become empowered to examine all fruit that comes our way. From there we act with purposeful vision and destiny- driven decisions. But first, we have to develop our emotional aptitude, which we'll call *apple*tude. Appletude is the ability to recognize our own issues, in order to tailor responses to achieve more powerful, destiny-driven outcomes. It positions us to *flip the script* on Fake-enstein thinking, recognize and root out Fake-enlies, and recalibrate focus toward purposeful outcomes that move you toward, instead of away from, destiny.

Finding Fakey

We have to find Fakey to root him out and we will need help. Since we are still wearing the Mosesitus blindfold we're not seeing straight. We need other folks to help. Remember, up to now the focus has been on the *wrong* self. It's time- out for our own take on the matter. We already see where all that leads. It's time to *see* we have a problem before we can *accept* that we have one, and there are no better eyes through which to face it than the eyes of those who have to live with Old Fakey. It includes attention to the personal growth it takes to build positive relationships along the Path of Purpose. Emotional appletude facilitates focus and ensures you are not still Mosesitus blind when you reach your own Promised Land border.

Applying the APPLE Inventory leverages our free choice and free will in taking control of powerful emotions before they cause us to self-destruct. To develop our appletude we have to first become fruit examiners. Note that I didn't say fruit inspectors. Inspectors hold the power to disqualify fruit as unfit. We do not have the power or the spiritual right to discount others because of their weaknesses. He calls us to compassion in that regard. We are merely examining it to see if it is ours (personal responsibility). If it is ours, we address the root by determining if the fruit can provide precious cider to sustain us along the Path of Purpose. We first have to determine which fruit belongs to us, and which belongs to others. We eliminate the bad while nurturing the good.

What's in Your Basket?

As fruit examiners, we learn to discern which apples are ours and which apples were sneaked into our harvests by people throwing phony seeds. We start where we are empowered — ourselves. Through that, we gain the ability to act appropriately when we observe bad fruit in others.

Imagine we are all walking around with baskets strapped to our waists. As we go through life in and out of relationships, people drop their fruit into our baskets. Depending on their character, people can toss good fruit or bad fruit into the same baskets into which we're dropping our own fruit. What if you could filter out the bad apples? What if you could refuse the bad apples or toss them out of the basket? What if you just closed the lid on your basket? Any one of these choices well placed can be beneficial.

However, just as with any good thing, out of proper balance it can defeat the purpose. With every good apple you block, you are missing vital fruit that sustains you along your Path of Purpose. That fruit might be a resource for others or a blessing for you. That is why self-isolation and ruined relationships are destiny-destroyers. Every aspect of our part in the Master plan includes coordinated assignments with and for others.

Lid Permanently Closed - Mission Impossible: If we close the lid completely, we are at risk of blocking good fruit. With the lid permanently closed, we cut off relationships without which it's impossible to execute the mission. Improper or complete lack of relationships with others is a destiny destroyer because it is through people that God accomplishes the Master Plan. Being caught up in the wrong relationships is a waste of precious time. Ruining good relationships blocks personal and spiritual growth. It's through relationships that God works out our characters. Isolation is a destiny destroyer. It can be beneficial to healing initially, but when it goes on too long, it is a likely ploy to keep us sidelined in the race toward destiny.

Lid Wide Open - Apple Toss: With the lid wide open, folks can willy-nilly grab and toss fruit at will. Your life is a toss-up, an apple toss! Your moods and emotions go along for the ride, jerking you around at will, all at the expense of the mission. Who you really are is anybody's guess because *you* surely have no clue. Fruit needs close examination to determine if it's good or bad. What looks like bad fruit can be the golden apple, if its nectar is properly tapped. The idea is to extract the wisdom out of each bad experience and apply it going forward.

It doesn't pay to just toss fruit. It's valuable to develop the skill and discernment to recognize which bad fruit will yield the nectar of wisdom and leverage that toward purpose and destiny, determine if it's yours or belongs to others, make the necessary adjustments to your own basket, and diligently protect its contents in the interest of purpose and destiny.

Lid Control - Leverage It: The lid on your basket swings both ways, so control what goes into your basket. Healing will bring you closer to who you really are, the person God sees, who He created you to be. With each shed layer of Fake-enstein you become more sensitive to God's direction. Rather than throwing out the baby with the bathwater, you will learn to throw out the bathwater and nurture the baby. You draw on the fruit that can provide wisdom's nectar, and know when to cut your losses and move on.

WHOSE APPLE IS IT, ANYWAY!

A friend one day asked what appeared to be an easy question: *"What does Santa Claus do at Christmas?"*

Trying to mask my impatience I said, *"He delivers presents."* What I was thinking was, Dude! Who doesn't know this? Are you out of decent conversation here?

But there was a not-so-obvious twist: "What else does he do?"

I had no response. Then he came with the obvious forehead slapper: *"He takes the milk and cookies,"* he smiled. He went on to explain that within every circumstance, every opportunity, every relationship, is a hidden treasure that we can take away from the experience.

I was so busy trying to figure out how a man as big as Santa could fit through anybody's chimney I failed to see how he got fat in the first place. The milk and cookies, of course! Life lessons learned are the milk and cookies -- the take-aways. They are the little pearls of wisdom we often overlook that are important to leverage on the Path of Purpose. These lessons are important because, without them we stagnate right where we are, or we move forward just to encounter yet another unwelcome opportunity to pick up on the lesson. If we learn the lesson, we progress forward toward destiny. If we fail to learn the lesson, we get stuck in that same cycle, making the same mistakes over and over.

Own It!

Remember when you were little and somebody called you a name? You'd turn it right back on them by saying, *"I know you are, but what am I?"* Okay, that's not going to work for us as adults because personal responsibility is not child's play, and the old ways we used to cope, as children, do not work for us as adults. We have to own our own behaviors. That requires seeing ourselves much more truthfully than we're used to. This is about accurate and honest self-examination to determine our own issues before bouncing all the blame onto others. So let's examine our fruit baskets. What's in yours?

Is the fruit fresh and luscious, inviting to whomever sees it? Is it rotten in places? Does it pass for good at a glance, but on further examination, it isn't? Are you asking, *"What is that one, and how did that get in here?"* Come on, you can be real with me. It's all between us. Check it with the APPLE Inventory — be real about it because you can only be as honest with others as you are with yourself. If you have heard the same complaint more than once from different people, it's a pretty sure bet you should start there.

Ask the Simple Question. What prompted this next self-realization was my complaining about being subjected to an unauthorized and unwelcome windshield washing by some homeless guy. I was lost, late, and angry. That's a lethal combination if you're not careful. The only thing that stood between me and a public altercation was the fact that I was in inner city Detroit, and I did have enough sense not to start clowning. If looks could take a person out, that man would be a goner. Right then, if my fifteen minutes of fame had to come on the front page of the Detroit Press, I was up for it! Headline: "Homeless Man Cold-Cocked by Mad Woman."

Sylvia always did lay it out just as it was: "*Why do you fly off the handle so easily? We have to figure out why you get so angry.*" That wasn't the first rightful chewing out I'd had from my former college roommate. Truth be told, she was always right and I deserved every minute of it. Yet, this time I threw out some denial-laced utterance and went on my angry way. To my mind, anytime I got angry was justified. To my mind, I didn't get angry any more than anybody else. I'd heard this before and shrugged it off every time. But when you get the same thing from so many different people, it behooves you to take stock and see if there is something to it.

I took a day off work to fast and figure out my major malfunction. I did a lot of listening that day. I wanted to hear God on the matter. He showed me how, even though I grew up in an intact family, I missed my daddy because he worked so hard. He would sometimes work double shifts to support the seven of us. Learning that my anger was rooted in what I perceived as an unmet need brought new clarity. I adjusted my thinking based on what I knew as an adult. Daddy and I even talked about it. I understood that from his perspective and upbringing that's what a man did to love his family; he worked. He provided. No matter what that entailed. To him it was love and being the man he knew to be. I loved him all the more for it.

That understanding brought the root of that anger into the here and now. It brought the clarity I needed in order to get about the business of recognizing Fake-enstein before he ran roughshod, wreaking havoc in my life. As a result, I got better. It wasn't overnight; it was a process. I would later learn there were more layers to uncover before I would gain full control.

No matter how I thought I had dealt with deep-seated grief, I was always sick. I was always in and out of the hospital having one medical procedure after another. A woman once told me it was because I was grieving over my children. I thought she was talking about being separated from my two living children. Apparently, that wasn't the case.

Shortly after leaving my first husband, I moved to Chicago where my aunt lived. She encouraged me to move there, agreeing to take care of my two children. I was destitute. I had lost my part-time job and had to borrow money from Sylvia for a one-way bus ticket. When I went to get my children to make the trip with me, my ex-husband had absconded to Detroit, taking both of them with him. I had to leave without them. My plans to go back for them were interrupted by a child abuse charge against my ex-husband and my daughter's hospitalization for failure to thrive. Those were the darkest days of my life.

During that time, I was back and forth to Detroit for hearings. In the first child custody hearing, my ex-husband admitted to the judge that he had abused me. That resulted in the children being split up between my parents, who raised my son, and my ex-husband's grandmother, who raised my daughter. When I came up pregnant about a year later, I was already a major basket case. The day I had that abortion was horrendous and indelibly etched in my psyche.

I was the last in line that day because my medical records indicated my emotional frailty. As I lay on that gurney outside the Cook County Hospital operating room, I heard the screams of woman after woman as they were herded through the surgery as if on an assembly line. But they weren't all woman. Some of them looked to be no older than thirteen. In the end, it was worse being last than it would have been going first. When it was my turn, I felt every bit of it — no anesthesia.

After it was over they rolled me into a huge ward where all those who went before me were already recovering. When it was time to leave, I dressed and headed into the rainy, cold, dreary afternoon, thinking how it was the perfect reflection of how I felt inside. As I headed down the subway steps, I stepped into a pool of blood. I wondered if it was from one of those little girls who just endured the trauma we shared. I can't think about that day without the vivid memory of that pool of blood.

The second abortion occurred because of a massive lower tract infection that had spread through my kidneys, womb, and ovaries. I was a mess. I was hospitalized for over a week because it took days to break the fever. I could have suffered through that pregnancy, but the man I was living with at the time was already on his way out. The morning I woke up with his gun in my face sealed his fate. Besides, I was not going to endure another hellacious pregnancy on his account. Had it not been for the hospitalization, I wouldn't have known I was pregnant.

I had my tubes tied right after that. The doctor was reluctant to do the operation on such a young woman. I was all of twenty years old at that time. But I convinced him that I couldn't emotionally endure another pregnancy, and I was not going to march into court pregnant while I was trying to get my children back. He did the deed. I stuffed it down, sucked it up, and moved on. So the day that strange woman told me I was grieving struck no chord with regard to the abortions.

Over a decade passed before I realized it was the two children I'd aborted that constantly haunted me. That grief bled right through my soul and set up camp in my body. A day of fasting and asking God about what was bugging me, and it all came to the forefront. From that day on the shackles were broken. I was free to move further along on my Path of Purpose.

The APPLE Inventory (attitude, perception, perspective, lies, and expectations) is an essential tool you will use repeatedly in all life situations. Check each aspect individually to determine if you might need to recalibrate your thinking. When in doubt, shut it down, get away by yourself, regroup, and apply the Inventory to measure your appletude.

Are you off focus? The APPLE Inventory will root out the truth as you develop new spiritual eyes that see past the fallout straight to the core of any matter.

Unforgiveness: Fatal Fruit

Forgiveness is at the root of inside out healing, and unforgiveness is Fakey's favorite meal. Remember, anything that nourishes Fakey represents spiritual malnutrition for you. You're starving out, my friend. No matter how egregious the wrong we endure, forgiveness is required. If there is something for which you have not forgiven others or yourself, you may have a good reason to be bitter, angry, and unforgiving, but the shed blood of Jesus says you have no right! If *He* has forgiven you, it serves no other purpose than self-punishment not to forgive yourself. It is dead weight not to forgive others. If He doesn't punish us, then who are *we* to exact punishment on ourselves or others?

God wants to restore you, make you whole. That's not going to happen by fighting Him at every turn. We have to get it into our heads that failure to forgive is not an option. Jesus forgives all kinds of sinners from the murderer to the molester, the thief to the liar. He forgives sins we do against Him and against each other. Some of the folks we are nurturing grudges against might have gotten saved by now and are moving along toward purpose. In God's eyes, their sin against you no longer exists. They have asked for forgiveness and are likely on their own paths of healing. Meanwhile, we are still strapped to the wrong they did to us. It's rotten seed that is yielding fatal fruit.

As good as God is, He also says we have to *bring* it to *get* it where forgiveness is concerned (see Mathew 6:14–15; Ephesians 4:32). When we cling to unforgiveness, we are holding on to the hurt as if letting go lets the wrongdoer off the hook. Unless you are sinless and walking around with huge nail holes in your extremities, you don't have the *authority* to let anybody off the hook; no sinner does. God and Jesus Christ hold that authority, and they have commanded us to forgive — not for His benefit, it's for our own good. Bottom line: your purpose and destiny are dependent on the commandment to forgive. While God certainly cares when He sees us making wrong choices, in the end it's no skin off *His* nose if we don't forgive others. It does, however, yield crop-choking, destiny-destroying weeds in our harvests.

After taking a reasonable amount of time to lick our wounds, we have to move forward. The first step in the process of forgiving takes deliberately seeking understanding. That means putting our own defenses in check long enough to ask God to show us that person, that situation or circumstance the way He sees it. Otherwise, we get caught up with somebody else's apples and wind up perpetuating their harm by allowing their rotten apples to contaminate our crop. Throwing bad fruit after bad can only lead to more bad. When we seek godly insight, we see the hurt that person suffered, the anguish they are in, the devastation they are trying to cover up. We look beyond the corpse to the core of the matter. We see past Fake-enlies to the root of any situation or circumstance as we develop discernment.

Will to Forgive

When my second husband was incarcerated, I struggled to forgive him. Without fail, as soon as I thought I had it licked, out of nowhere some residual drama would set me off. Sometimes over little or nothing, Fakey-Jake would hijack my whole day. I was all caught up on every level, and once Old Fakey was unleashed, there was no coming back from it. It generally meant my whole day was ruined. That's the state I was in, one day, as I sat seething over a meeting delay. Every bit of anger was evident in my demeanor. I was not a happy camper and everybody in the building knew it. As I sat there seething, in walked five-foot-nothing of pure-D power and glory. I'm sure she had been well warned of the mad monster who awaited her. Yet, smile unbroken, her presence defied, indeed neutralized, all that.

"Hi. I'm Mary Anne Claywell!"

I'm telling you this woman was glory walking. Some people just exude the glory of God in their presence, and the whole atmosphere changes. We became fast friends. She was a divine connection. Mary Ann helped me understand that forgiveness is not a magic wand that waves away the hurt. *"Linda, you will to forgive, and then you allow the Lord to heal your heart."*

"Get out of here! You mean to tell me" . . . wait a minute . . . I had to pull myself together. Hold up, you're telling me that my still hurting doesn't mean I haven't forgiven? My still struggling doesn't mean I haven't forgiven? Wow, I had it all confused. I thought because I was still going through emotional turmoil I hadn't forgiven. So forgiveness and healing are two different things, and forgiveness is the catalyst to healing. You can't heal from the inside out without forgiveness, and forgiveness naturally leads to healing. Again, note that we *will* to forgive. That concept is a key player in the "war strategy" we discuss in more detail further on. While forgiveness is a decision, it is also a three-step process: 1) seek understanding; 2) understanding leads to compassion; and 3) compassion leads to forgiveness.

- *Understanding*: Remember that Old Fakey has us Mosesitus blind so we have to get input from trusted sources outside ourselves. It's the only way to get past our blindness. From our own perspectives, the situation might appear one way. Yet at the core, it is a different story. Get this information before giving place to irrational emotional discharges. Understanding lies in the backstory at the core of the matter.
- *Compassion*: Understanding softens our hearts, allowing us to relate to others on levels we can't reach because of our own denial. As we see past Fake-enstein, we see people as God sees all of us. He sees past the corpses we are dragging around. He sees past the defenses and the fear He knows we have endured, but it doesn't cloud or change His plan for us. He loves us past all that.
- *Forgiveness:* God doesn't categorize sin. He forgives, forgets (Isaiah 43:25), and restores (Psalm 103:12). He said He forgives and

forgets. He commands that we forgive each other, but He never commanded that we forget. Forgiveness doesn't mean we ever forget the offense. What it does is free us up to leverage the lessons learned by drawing appropriate boundaries with others and ourselves. It moves us into healing and allows us to leverage what we have learned to help or mentor others going through the same thing. The idea is to learn from our mistakes and move on along the Path of Purpose.

Forgiveness is a deal breaker where purpose, vision, and destiny are concerned. Nobody gets a pass on it, no matter how egregious the wrong endured.

Forgiveness: Deal Breaker

Immaculée Ilibagiza, a Rwandan genocide survivor who, after three months crowded in a 3-foot x 4-foot bathroom with six other women, immerged to find her entire family, parents, grandparents, and three brothers murdered. "*Instead of letting rage, grief, and a desire for revenge take over her life, Immaculée reached inside herself and found only forgiveness.*" [9] That's because God required it of her. She did it even though she didn't understand it. Because she focused and depended on God during the ordeal, her heart was full of desire to do whatever He asked of her. Understand or not, she forgave. During that process, she developed compassion for her enemies.

She started praying for them. That released the power of God in the middle of trying circumstances. When she finally got free, she found streets full of rotting bodies, a French rescue team that abandoned her in the face the enemy and her own crossroads to destiny that found her face to face with the death and hatred that destroyed everything she loved.

As she stood there staring down death, she had a decision to make — death or destiny? Choosing to believe God, she spoke out of her very spirit to that evil, and her attacker dropped his machete. She led a procession of survivors straight through the middle of enemy forces unscathed. Any of that sound familiar? Does it remind you of the Exodus? Immaculée's journey to freedom started with compassion and forgiveness. Facing down hatred, bitterness, and fear, she believed God. She set aside her desire for retribution. She traded the machete of hatred and bitterness for destiny.

We see the opposite with some families of crime victims who seek "closure" through execution of the guilty party. Somehow, they see those events as the culmination of the healing process. They feel they cannot move on until "justice is done." Their focus is retribution as the point of relief from crippling grief. I wonder how many awaken the next day to find themselves still facing the same anger, confusion, and bitterness. That's because healing is a journey, a process that is never predicated upon any external event.

The perpetrator might live or not live. They might get their just deserts or not. We might get to see justice served or we may not. Regardless, none of that will ever erase the pain of victimization. We have to walk it out. We have to progress through it. But, as long as we hold on to anger, bitterness, offense, lack of forgiveness, and hurt, either by denying their existence or repeatedly replaying the hurtful event, we cannot move forward. Healing begins by leveraging the will to forgive. After we have forgiven, we are back on our Path of Purpose. The Path of Purpose is paved with healing. That healing goes as deep as the wound – or as deep as we let it. After we have forgiven and embarked on our healing journey, it's time to start honing our harvest.

Chapter 4: Hone Your Harvest

Forgiveness is the catalyst to healing, and the power of choice is the catalyst to breaking old patterns. Incorporating the APPLE Inventory will root out blind spots in our character. Now we develop our own war strategy to identify the mindfields in which the irrational emotional discharges (IED) are lurking. We are about to position ourselves so that the enemy can no longer take us by surprise. We have to alter our perceptions to make sure we are planting toward a better future harvest that aligns with what God has planned for us — our destiny. Let's develop a game plan for sidestepping the mindfields that trigger knee- jerk, destiny-destroying, emotional responses.

Triggers

Triggers are personalities, people, places, circumstance, or things that set off strong emotional responses and drive you to react irrationally. Triggers can set off the IEDs that lurk in mindfields set up to keep us off focus. The split second between pulling the trigger (the event) and discharge (the response or behavior that results) is where we are going to focus. With firearms, pulling the trigger is the point of no return. Once that bullet discharges, it's headed for its intended target. However, when something triggers an IED, we can intervene. We don't have to allow it to ruin our lives. We can leverage our wills to stop the destruction it can cause. We don't have to give in to it.

The things that cause irrational emotions are usually based in some past negative life experience. When we don't recognize these triggers, we can become enslaved to them. We have to educate ourselves regarding what triggers our IEDs before we can dig down to see in what they are rooted. Once we know that, we can develop a game plan to stop them in their tracks. The time between the trigger (event) and our response (sown seed) is where we leverage our wills. This is a critical point of intervention. Getting this right makes the difference between sowing toward destiny and sowing toward the same old crop we've been getting. So let's make ourselves a trigger list. Take a minute to think back over your life. Make a list of every recurring theme you find. Categorize those under three headings: personalities, situations, and things.

Personalities (People)

Which people irk you? Is there a certain type of personality that sets you off? Pay particular attention to any situation in which you experience an immediate dislike for someone you meet. Is it intuition or something else? Never subjugate true intuition to anybody or anything. Every time I broke this rule, I regretted it. For some reason, no matter how strong the intuition was, I would do all I could to ignore it. It never served me well. I've finally learned to embrace it as God's way of telling me to avoid future heartache or impending danger. It took a lot of healing before I learned how to leverage rather than run from it. But, once you determine that the matter is not due to intuition, you have to set about questioning yourself about of whom, in your past, this personality or person reminds you.

Beware, however, of using intuition as an excuse for claiming you don't like somebody. Until you're skilled at recognizing Old Fakey (defense mechanisms) before he sets off an IED, you will need to examine whether it's actually a "check" in your spirit or if it's really because you have deep-seated issues you need to root out. It's very easy to be fooled in this regard unless you recognize truth.

Facing the Truth

I used to have very few, if any, female friends. I told myself it was because I'm not into drama and backstabbing. My phone hardly rang because I could find better things to do with my time than chitchat about nothing or belly ache about my problems just to get off the phone having to face the same old issues with no evident solution. I wasn't into man bashing, gossip, or catfights. I just had better things to do — at least that's what I told myself. But, here is the backstory.

My issue went back to a little ten or eleven-year-old girl, who spent days working up the nerve to tell her mother she wanted a closer relationship with her. From my perspective, there was always tension between me and my mother. I was always getting chewed out for stuff that made no sense to me. I just couldn't understand why she always seemed to be mad at me. I wanted to get along with my mother, and I didn't want us to be unable to talk outside of her routine lectures about how fat I was, what I could or couldn't wear, or how I was inappropriately dressed. I had no clue I was walking around in a woman's body. I was just a little girl who wanted to wear miniskirts and bell-bottoms with the rest of my classmates. I wanted an end to it, and I couldn't find the nerve to tell her that I needed her and wanted to get along better.

One night, on one of our fourteen-mile drives to the nearest grocery store, I got it out. I don't remember the words I used, but her reaction is indelible. She said something about not getting along with her mother when she was growing up, so she basically expected nothing more between us because that's how it is between moms and daughters. That was that. I was shocked and deeply hurt.

I carried that around for decades until a therapist pointed out the connection between that incident and the fact that I didn't have female relationships. Even in the face of that truth, I didn't make the connection between that and my purpose. I had to chew on it for a while before accepting that, yes, I was scared to get hurt, and I associated all women with my mother!

Situations (Circumstances)

What situations trigger strong emotional reactions for you? Painful events and trauma generally make submitting to authority a challenge. Is this case with you? Are there other situations that seem to trigger recurring emotional themes? I am still struggling with IEDs in this regard. As much as I know better, this thing consistently seems to take me off focus.

I have a major issue with being falsely accused. When I was accused of something while growing up, I wasn't allowed to explain myself or deny my involvement. I internalized that frustration. It still affects me. In the face of a false accusation, I cry. On the surface, I'm an articulate and confident professional. Yet one false accusation and I'm off and running. I cry every time I perceive I'm being misunderstood or falsely accused without opportunity for rebuttal. In every single case, that frustrated, angry, little girl takes over (Fake-enstein). It takes forever to stuff her back inside. But stuffing her isn't the answer because she just keeps popping up.

Instead of reacting to current events as if looking up at my mother and biting my tongue, I need to remember in that moment that I'm not eight years old, these folks are not my mother, and being frustrated and angry isn't the answer. I perceive myself in that moment as that little girl instead of acting as an adult. If leadership is my destiny, then that falsely accused little girl is a roadblock. She's throwing mud on my lenses to set me up for misperception. Until she's properly dealt with, I could move into leadership on knowledge, skill, and ability, yet do a lousy job of it because I'm seeing myself as a misunderstood little girl. It's living in the past.

Things

An inanimate object can mean all things good to one person, and trigger fear in the next. It's the meanings we attach to things that make the difference. The aroma of fresh, homemade bread wafting through the air can trigger warm childhood memories of grandmother, safety, and innocence for one person. For another, it can be an aversion. If fresh, homemade bread was wafting through the air during a painful life event, that smell could trigger negative emotions even without the person knowing why. Are there things that cause strong negative reactions for you? Add them to the list.

CNN reporter, Soledad O'Brien, tweeted about her Black in America series the other day, and it set off considerable discussion as people related their childhood memories of something they were told they couldn't do because they were black. One person talked about being told to pinch her nose in order to make it smaller, less wide. It reminded me of a pink-and- white dress my great grandmother gave me. I loved that dress. My mother didn't. She told me I was too dark to wear pink. I still don't wear pink.

These are examples of how we are affected by life and how one well- placed negative statement can engrain itself for life. In both of these examples, pinching the nose and wearing pink, we were affected by our parents' views of themselves, such as their skin color or physical traits. We were too young to understand that these beliefs were rooted in our parents' upbringings, their own life experiences. They were unaware of how their expressing those perceptions would affect us. As you create your trigger list, be mindful of patterns and themes that evolve. These nuances are a roadmap to common causes of various triggers. An example of this is the fact that people carrying deep trauma develop distrust for others, including those in authority over them. That doesn't jibe with purpose, and it surely won't end up with the destiny God intended. We don't serve a God of confusion, and there are authorities in place to keep the order. All of us have to fall in with our specific places in the Master Plan. The only one in the mix without a boss is God. So when we buck against authority, we're off the Path of Purpose and need to recalibrate how we're thinking.

Take your time creating the list of triggers. It should be comprehensive. As you go through your daily routine, write down the people, situations, and things that cause negative emotions. Leave nothing out. The list is meant to increase your self-awareness. As you consistently apply the APPLE Inventory and the FRUITS Philosophy (discussed later in this chapter) whenever you experience a trigger, you will gain understanding of why these things are a problem for you. As you learn the root of these issues and seek God's guidance in healing from them, you will find yourself crossing them off the list one at a time.

List of Truthful and Trusted Others

Start another list. At the top, write "God." He is your first line of defense against false thinking, and He is the truth you need to seek. He is the go-to Guy who knows you inside out. He is the one to go to when you need a reality check.

Now continue the list by adding "People I Trust" to tell you the truth about yourself. List all those you can think of who have demonstrated they truly have your best interests at heart. These can be family members, friends, ministers, or anybody you have known long enough to have experience with how they relate to you. It is important, as well, to observe how they live their own lives. I'm not saying you should look for perfect people. I am saying that people's lives reveal how they view the world, how they think, and how well they have overcome their own pasts. So what they went through in the past is not the focus. The focus is how they are living in the here and now.

Beware of people who counsel you out of their own unresolved issues. Statements such as, "*I would have . . .*" or "*If that were me I would have . . .*" are often warning signs. If their first response to your situation is highly emotionally charged, it might be a sign of Fake-enstein in full effect. These statements are not always, in themselves, signs of a problem. It is easy to tell if these people are reacting out of their own unresolved issues if their emotions appear out of sync with the matter or problem at hand.

For example, let's say you mention to a couple of coworkers that you had an argument with your spouse. You relate your side of the story. Coworker #1 responds with various context-related questions and presents you with several possibilities that help you to see how your spouse might be thinking, or how he or she might have viewed the events leading up to the argument.

Coworker #2, without asking any questions, takes your side with a highly emotionally charged response, telling you what you ought to do and berates your spouse with statements peppered with, "*I would'a,*" *You should'a,*" or "*If it were me,*" statements.

Coworker #1 responded much more objectively than Coworker #2. The first coworker challenged your way of thinking about the matter, thus encouraging you to consider other ways to view the situation. Therefore, Coworker #1 is the type of individual you should consider adding to your list of trusted others. Remember, this is not supposed to be someone who will coddle your wrong ways of thinking. This should be someone who challenges you to hold your perceptions, and therefore your perspectives, to the light of truth. This should be someone who can lend a listing ear without judgment while encouraging you to recognize where your thinking does not align with truth.

Consider including on your list, individuals who are spiritually aligned with their own Paths of Purpose. Anytime you can add someone who has been where you are, made similar mistakes, and came through it able to talk about it, do it! There is a certain level of healing that comes along with a person's being able to talk about their past.

Once your trusted others list is created, go back over it. Add anybody else who comes to mind after reading through the FRUITS Philosophy (below). As you grow spiritually and heal emotionally, you can expect many revisions to your trusted others list. The idea is to weed out everybody you know who won't be completely truthful with you. The list should only contain those who love you enough to push through their own defenses, to see and tell you the hardcore truth.

The FRUITS Philosophy

Now we need a game plan to counteract our trigger-happy habits and initiate the change that will put us back on track. But first, we must examine our fruit. To be fruit examiners we need a mind toward an ultimate goal, our assigned mission in the Master Plan. The road to our own Promised Land is paved with purposeful focus and destiny-driven decisions. That means when we fly off into our scripts we have to rein it in and initiate a personal inventory to determine where it's coming from and why. With practice, it will be easier to apply this method before flying into destiny-destroying behaviors.

The FRUITS Philosophy is a step-by-step process you can apply as you move through your healing journey. We are going to *flip the script* on old ways of thinking and behaving. We are going to *recalibrate* our perceptions through the *understanding* we gain from *investigating* all aspects of the challenge, interpreting the results, and initiating a purposeful game plan. Finally, we will learn to *trust* the process and *stay tuned* by developing a teachable spirit sensitive to God's direction.

Step 1: Flip the Script

Bottom line: God wrote His script for you. From which script are you operating? Rule number one in script flipping: do not jump to conclusions; flip the script on that old behavior. Just tear it up, throw it away, and start rewriting your life. If, in the moment, you are unsure of the proper actions, generally doing the opposite of what you usually do is the ticket. Otherwise, when in doubt be quiet. You don't want to have to take back any regretful statements. Based on knowing old patterns have not been working, shut them down before they leave your mouth. Think. Is this another item that belongs on your list of situations, personalities, or things that typically set you off? Fight it! Don't go with that flow. Refuse to go along with the emotional status quo and stop the minute those old emotions and responses are triggered. Go no further. It's time for some serious self-evaluation.

As soon as you can, excuse yourself from the conversation, or back away from the situation in order to challenge your thoughts. In professional situations, it might mean politely or assertively excusing yourself. In personal relationships, you might have to agree to a "call word" or gesture that means time out or back off. For example, you might use the words time out, or you might say, "*Stop*" or have an agreed-upon hand gesture. Make sure that both parties agree to the chosen phrase or gesture and set ground rules around how long a cooling off period is allowed. For this to work, both parties must agree to how each must respond to the agreed-upon statement or gesture. That way use of it should not result in either party being offended by it.

Remember, this is not a license for rudeness, and it should not be done strictly because you don't want to hear what the other party has to say. Instead, it's time that allows you to work through any irrational emotional discharges IEDs before they detonate. It is time for you to take a minute to challenge the seed of your own thinking before it results in planting (sowing) toward a negative outcome (harvest).

If you are in a professional setting or situation, your responses have to reflect professional conduct. If something is said or done that triggers your responses, you should wait for an appropriate point in the conversation to ask for clarification of the matter. In doing that, be aware of your tone. We often are unaware of how we sound to others. Once you obtain the clarification, you might request an opportunity to discuss the matter further at a later time. By doing so you allow yourself the opportunity to see it from all sides and return with a more objective response.

In other cases you might say something such as, "I'm very interested in a productive discussion on this. And I'd like to take some time to think about how we might reach an effective conclusion to the matter that would work for all of us."

If the discussion is heated, and the person with whom you are speaking is emotional, you could say, *"Perhaps its better that we discuss this later when we have all cooled down enough to have a more productive conversation."* Sometimes you just have to ask the other person to stop, excuse yourself, and go calm down. Once you've got a grip on yourself, move right into Step 2.

Step 2: Recalibrate

Our frame of reference needs recalibrating. To calibrate means to adjust our point of view to a specific standard in order to check the accuracy of our perceptions. We've already determined that our focus is off. It's time to hold those old beliefs to a higher standard. This sounds easier than it is. In the middle of an emotional discharge, it can be difficult to regain composure. Decide up front that you won't wallow in those negative emotions. The temptation is to nurture their familiarity. It's a mindfield. Don't go that way! Instead, apply these rules:

Recalibration Rule 1: Don't engage negativity. Don't engage negativity in yourself, and don't engage negativity in others. This applies to all possible situations and circumstances. It means the minute you recognize negative self-talk (scripts), shut it down, and replace it with truth! Find an applicable scripture to replace it with, or find a scriptural affirmation to use. It's not enough to stop the negative thought; you have to replace it with something positive and true.

If the negativity comes from someone else, disengage immediately. Don't take that apple. If you notice that someone you know is always complaining, always blaming others for their own mess, always making fun of others or being otherwise negative, it's bad apples that you don't need to bring into your harvest. Recognize it as such, refuse it, and move on. In the interest of not engaging negativity in yourself, don't get caught up with judging their behaviors. It is not ours to judge, and every moment spent in judgment of others is a moment off purposeful focus for us.

There is no need to fool yourself. Being around that negativity is poison, and nurturing it in *you* is destiny-lethal. It is important to surround yourself with anything and everything purpose related. Remember the water- seeks-its-own-level analogy. Negativity breeds negativity, and it will surely bear a negative harvest in your life.

Our sphere of control *excludes* everyone but *us*. Until we get our own sphere of control in order, we are ill equipped to influence others in a positive way. Remember this rule to keep yourself on track.

Recalibration Rule 2: Beware when others trigger negativity in you. Update your trigger list each time you discover something new. Then employ the APPLE Inventory to root out the core cause of that reaction. Don't assume that every trigger is an indication that someone else is wrong. That conclusion will be drawn after the APPLE Inventory self-assessment. Whatever the final outcome, always remember that you can't control others; you can only control yourself. Remember to ask God the simple question, "What is *my* major malfunction?"

Recalibration Rule 3: Always remember that your own perceptions can be off. An innocent statement or gesture could trigger painful emotions without the other person even knowing it. So what's perceived as negative might look completely different by the time you work through the FRUITS Philosophy. The temptation is to assume the other person is the one who is wrong. The fact is, no matter whether they are wrong or right, it could be you who is off. Whether that person is wrong or right, it's your responsibility to root out the truth in the matter and act on that truth.

Step 3: Understanding

This step is where the transformation begins. It's time to gather facts and process what you have discovered. This is where honest self-evaluation is required as you consider the other side of the story. In this phase, your perceptions are challenged at their core. Mosesitus (denial) blinds and desensitizes us to truth. It's the Fake-enstein effect. Under its influence, we don't see the impact of our behaviors on others. Part of personal responsibility is becoming more self-aware, which includes understanding the difference between the intent of our actions and their actual impact.

Intent vs. Impact. Intent and impact can be divergently opposed. Our way of seeing things isn't necessarily everybody's way of seeing things. Understanding this is job number one. It's the beginning of truth. Just as we are prone to Mosesitus, so are the other people we deal with daily. So you could say, "whoop-de-*doo*" to somebody, who will swear you said, "whoop- dee-*da*." From there the whole conversation takes a defensive turn that ends in an unnecessary misunderstanding. Our best intentions will never outweigh the actual impact of our behaviors. Let me say that again. *Our best intentions will not outweigh the impact of our behaviors* on others and ourselves. Therefore, whether we *meant* to come off wrong or not, if we *did* come off that way, explaining our good intentions after the fact doesn't change the end result. Beware of the communication chasm.

The Chasm. Impact overrules intent because impact drives results. So if you didn't get your intended results from an action (behavior, communication, gesture), it's likely due to the Fake-enstein effect. Picture an imaginary see-through tube between you and the person with whom you're communicating. We'll call them the receiver. One end of the tube is over your mouth; the other end of the tube is over the receiver's ear. As you talk, your sentences float word by word through the tube and into the ear of the receiver. The tube represents the gap between our intended message and the way it is received (perceived). If the receiver hears the wrong message, your intended outcome might be disappointing. At that point, it doesn't matter what you said; what matters is the message they received.

Here's how it works. You say, "*Go turn the stove off under the eggs.*" Instead, they turned in and went to bed. Your kitchen's flaming, and you're berating the poor receiver, who is guilty of nothing more than acting on his best understanding of your message. Put yourself in the other person's shoes. Was he reacting to some negativity you communicated in your attitude or tone? Was there a miscommunication or misunderstanding that caused things to get off on the wrong track? If so, what was it, and what's the backstory? How do others' observations line up with yours? If they don't line up, consider how your thinking might need some revision. What was really going on with you?

This chasm exists because we all operate out of our own life experiences, and those experiences are as diverse as the people who hold them. It is important to remember that most of us have some form of Fake-enstein operating, and we are all prone to mindfields. Recognizing this goes a long way toward gaining the understanding it takes to disarm IEDs before they blow up in our faces. Once an IED detonates, the cleanup can be time consuming. Failure to disarm that discharge might cost you divine connections due to ruined relationships.

It takes more effort to regain ground than to maintain it. Remember to focus on the desired outcome, don't take things personally, and understand that not every negative reaction is about the current situation or circumstance. It can often be about yours and/or somebody else's past.

Step 4: Investigate, Interpret, Initiate

Up to now, you have probably developed relationships that don't challenge your blindness or upset Fake-enstein's equilibrium. This information- gathering phase has to include the perspectives of people who will tell you the unadulterated truth. In this phase, consider adding to the list someone you never go around because you already know that the truth is exactly what you'll get. These people would generally be offensive to your Fake- enstein. That's exactly the type of people you need as FRUIT consultants. As long as they can keep confidences and have your best interest at heart, go back now and add them to your list of trusted and truthful others.

Investigate

Run the situation by various other observers of the triggering event. If you have to contact someone who was not involved, do not color the narrative with perceptions. Simply deliver the facts cold: no interpretation or innuendo on your part. This will take some practice. The point of this phase of the FRUITS Philosophy is to help develop your listening skills. In this phase, you are not allowed to defend or rationalize your own perceptions. This is where you hear and listen to numerous other perspectives. Note that I said hear *and* listen. You have to hear in order to listen. Hearing is a step we often skip because Fake-enstein doesn't want to hear truth.

- *Listen Twice, Speak Half that Much or Not at All.* Fake- enstein makes for a lousy listener, and when we're caught up like that, we're not aware of how much we're missing. In this phase, the goal is to gather as much outside information as possible. This is fact finding to establish an objective measure of the situation. The idea is gathering outside information, not rehashing the offense. Most of this time is spent listening. You are allowed to ask clarifying questions. Defending your position is off limits. At first, this is uncomfortable, and you're going to struggle not to interject. Old Fakey isn't giving up without a fight, and every time someone says something you don't like, he's rushing in at full force; count on it. Don't go with that. Fight that feeling.

- *Truer Picture*. In the final days of my second marriage, I was hospitalized for an emotional breakdown. That followed my learning that my husband had molested my teenage daughter. Added to that was the sudden loss of my dearest pet and mind-numbing emotional stress so oppressive I lost a whole day. To this day, I still can't figure out where that day went.

During the psychological assessment, the psychologist noted that I needed to "internalize self-esteem." What? First, I wasn't aware I *had* any at that point, and second, what self-esteem I had wasn't externally driven (from my own vantage point). To add insult to that injury, another therapist insisted on placing me in the trauma group just because there was rape in my background. I'll clean up how I responded to that like this: "Look, I'm here to get over this mind-bending depression. Those rapes are old news, I'm over them. Just help me cope with this God-forsaken mess of a marriage so I can function enough to go back to work." Can you say, "Stuffing"? In yet another instance, during my internship in graduate school, my clinical supervisor insisted I make regular therapy sessions part of my learning plan because, when I walked into the room, she felt "trauma." Get that? Not drama . . . trauma. Others are in a better position to explain how they experience us. When we get the same response from so many different people, it behooves us to take stock and see if there is something to it. Even though I didn't see what they were talking about, I asked the Lord what I call the "simple question."

- Ask the Simple Question. I took the day off to fast and seek God about whatever my major malfunction was. With me, the couple of times this happened the Lord clearly showed me the root issues. Thankfully that was all it took. I don't remember having any major game plan for getting better as a result of it, but there was power in finally knowing the root of the fallout. From there on it was a case-by-case, situation-by-situation matter of doing what He told me to do.

Every behavior is rooted in some past experience. We may not even be aware of what happened to us, let alone how it informs our perspectives, thoughts, and behaviors. So it's best to just cut to the chase by asking God the simple question: what is my major malfunction? In other words, where is this problem coming from, Lord? Why do I keep doing this? Ask Him to show you the core issues and quit beating yourself up over the fallout. Stop majoring on minors by repeatedly wrestling with the symptoms of a problem, and cut straight to the core issues... the cure is in the cause. In this phase of the process, the power lies in what we learn about ourselves.

Interpret

This is where you'll consider all the information you received. It's out of this evaluation that we will devise a plan to achieve our desired outcomes.

- *Process the Information.* Breaking through how we have convinced ourselves that we are not affected by things is the greatest challenge to this part of the process. Just like the children of Israel who stood face to face with destiny and were disqualified before they could enter, you have to know you *have* a problem to know you *are* the problem. As you process what you have learned, you have to resist the urge to disregard the sound opinions of trusted others.

This is where Old Fakey will have a fit! He'll creep into your analysis if you let him. Refocus on the information at hand, and when those Fake-enlies are flying, shut them down. Remember anything coming from Old Fakey is false reality. It's not true. It's not real. Focus on the information with an open mind and compare it to how you interpreted the event. It's all of this information in tandem that brings you closer to the truth of the matter. If the consensus is that you are justified in your interpretation of the events, you don't get to address it as you used to do. You have to devise a different approach, starting with the outcome you want. Then get with God for further guidance. Be sure to ask for wisdom, the proper words, and the appropriate time to discuss the matter with the offender. However, if the consensus concludes that you are way off track, go back to the simple question section above. It's going to take a shift in your thinking about it.

- *One Time at the Right Time.* Now that you have conducted an objective analysis, it's time to seek wise counsel about *what* to say, *how* to say it, and *when* to say it. Sometimes you'll still be working through your emotions. This is a time of healing, reflection, and attitude adjustment, but this time it's from the inside out. We are used to slapping on bandages and concocting surface solutions to soothe ourselves. But, inside-out healing is an ongoing process. To be avoided at all cost are the old ways of thinking, talking, and behaving. So you have to move in God's timing, not when you want to. That means that you act on any truth in the situation before confronting the situation or the offender. In addressing the matter with the offender, it is best to do so after processing through the emotional fall out. It has to be done objectively and it has to be done in love.

There was a woman with whom I worked who just got on my last nerve. We could not communicate. I consider myself well spoken, and so was she. But when it came to communicating with one another, forget about it. She was also extremely controlling and demanding — two behaviors on my own Trigger List. One day she went way too far with that mess, and it was all I could do to back away. I had already learned to shut it down in the middle of high emotions. I hadn't yet learned how to categorize whose apples were whose

That thing got to me so badly that I would have vivid dreams of cursing her out. The dreams were so real it was a major disappointment when I'd wake up. I remember exactly where I was when the Lord finally spoke to me about it, saying, Linda, that might make you feel better but it won't help her. As always when He speaks to me, a few simple words spoke volumes. That was one of my first it's-not-about-you lessons. That argument was just the apple. It took months to root out my issues and walk through that healing.

The deepest wisdom spoken at the wrong time is unwise. The words spoken at the right time need to be said only once to gain effect. As president of a local chapter of the National Treasury Employee Union (NTEU), I oversee an executive board of chapter leaders. One day I got a call from the executive vice president, who proceeded to ream me out over a litany of complaints. Within five minutes, I had been accused of neglecting the chapter, favoritism, and you name it. I just listened. The insult to that injury was that she ended it by telling me she had summarily cut a backroom deal with an administrator that compromised the bargaining unit. I just listened, said goodbye, and hung-up.

I learned a long time ago that whether a person brings it wrong or not, I have a responsibility to the truth in the message. I focused on that first. Knowing I'm not a detail-oriented person, I started paying closer attention to my administrative responsibilities, got our meetings back on track, and paid attention to where folks might need more direction. It was weeks before I addressed the matter of her wrong because that had to be placed on hold until I addressed the truth in her message.

In the meantime, I continued to speak with her off and on as business required. During those contacts, I never broached the subject of the accusatory call. However, one day I knew it was time. The message was straightforward, emphatic, and without emotion. Addressing the backstory on her part, I told her that I was not her father or her former supervisors, and I would appreciate her dealing with me on the basis of my own character. I proceeded to thank her for the truthful part of her complaint and assured her that I would never engage in any retaliatory actions against her. I ended it by telling her I did not appreciate the way she addressed me and that it could not happen again.

Had I responded out of my initial emotions, that relationship would have been ruined because I would have given her exactly what her *Fake-* enstein perpetuated — drama and dissention. I would have been just as wrong as she was. By waiting until the right time to respond, I said it *one* time, at the *right* time. We'll never have to have that discussion again.

Initiate

All the investigation and interpretation means nothing until you initiate action based on what you learn. That means what you learn about yourself in the process has to guide you going forward. In other words, live what you learn. If that requires you to apologize to someone, do it. If it means you have to make some adjustments in your behaviors, make it so. If it means you were right in how you saw the situation, and it turns out they were wrong, follow God's leading in when and how you address it.

Remember you have to give mercy to get mercy, and you still don't get to judge. Sometimes it will take a period of healing before you will be allowed to say something to that person. Sometimes you won't be allowed to address it. However it shakes out; remember the one-time-at-the-right- time rule. If you work through your issues first, you will gain the necessary discernment to hear God's direction. We do more harm than good when we act out of emotions. Address the truth in what you learned and follow God's guidance in initiating the plan.

WHOSE APPLE IS IT, ANYWAY!

Step 5: Trust the Process

When you upset the applecart, chaos follows. When you start applying these principles, you can count on some relationships falling by the wayside. Whether the relationship is platonic or romantic, you have to remember that some, if not most, of your current relationships are based on your Fake- enstein personality. These folks have only seen glimpses of the true you. So when you begin to act foreign to them, their Fake-enstein is fighting for its existence and likely cannot tolerate the true you without a backlash.

Their Fake-enstein is fighting back tooth and nail, clambering around in the dark trying to find the old equilibrium. Less and less can they find that person you *thought* you were. When Old Fakey can't find that, he acts out, acts up, and heads out to lunch. You'll see extreme behaviors that will surprise you because the healthier you become, the more ridiculous and outlandish they will seem. When you see this going on, grab a cup of tea or coffee, sit back, and feel good about the fact that it's working!

Your eyes are finally open, you are back on track with purpose, and you have outgrown that acquaintance. You are no longer stuck on stupid. You are progressing toward the Border of Destiny. You're gaining focus, and eventually you will gain sight of the vision as you become acquainted with your True Self.

In consistency lies the power. It took years, maybe decades, to get where you are. You didn't develop those defenses overnight, and it will take determination to turn it around. Applied consistently, it becomes easier, and as you learn of your True Self, you realign with your Path of Purpose.

Step 6: Stay Tuned

Ten pages into a scathing letter to a boyfriend, I just threw up my hands and thought, *When do I get to reap my harvest? I've sown enough unconditional love in my life. I'm tired! When do I get to have a healthy relationship? Where is the reciprocity? How much more do I have to give before I can finally see a return on that investment? What?* Uh, oh! Oh no! I didn't really expect Him to answer. He wanted me to stay with the man! "Really, Lord? Another what-did- I-tell-you-to-do lesson? Whhhhy?"

It's what I would do. His cucumber-cool response brought no comfort. Great. The one person in the universe who can stand on do-what-I-say *and* do-what-I-do just called me out. A lot of thoughts went through my mind during the ensuing pregnant pause, not the least of which was, Well . . . I'm not You! I let go of that one fast. When I came to my emotional senses, I was in an all-too-familiar place: another crossroads. I had been here before. So I cut out the losing-battle wrestling match I used to go through between the direction and the decision.

"So I get to learn the same lesson again, huh?" By the time I finished shaking my head, I got it. *"Okay, I get it: you learn the lesson once, and then you get multiple opportunities to utilize it — a spiritual internship, so to speak. Slowly exhaling a deep breath, I settled in. If that's what it will take to get through to him . . . I asked for Your wisdom in this situation, and now I have to act right."* More boot camp for me! Yay.

It was only a few months before I was wanting out of that deal. I didn't care about what that meant, and I was ready to take the consequences like a man. I didn't care. I was through and fed up, and I was not going to be where I clearly wasn't wanted. The whole time I was going through that, I knew that inside the fear was flying. So I was struggling with these things:

1. Seeing some of the same warning signs, I had seen in my last marriage and fighting to push through my *Fake*-enstein to sort out how much of my perception was fear and how much was real.
2. Trying not to overextend the sorting-out phase as a means of avoiding the inevitable.
3. Wondering whether I was *strong* enough to end it.
4. Wrestling with the disobedience of, and having the unmitigated gall to, tell God what I wasn't going to do: clearly defiance and clearly out of fear.
5. Wondering if maybe the time had run out on this assignment. Note I said "assignment" because, from the moment he told me to stay that was what it had been for me, an *assignment* within the mission. Pitiful, huh?

The day came that I felt a release from this assignment…it happened the day the man calmly looked me in the eyes and said, "I'm not gonna change." The day that relationship ended, it ended for good and it ended with my knowing I had given my all with no regrets. I'm glad to be free and I'm at peace for the effort because of the lessons learned. When you come through your first battle victoriously, you'll feel as if there is nothing in the world you can't conquer. What could be worse than what you just found your way out of? Whatever other challenges arise, you will feel as though you have it all in spades, and you're ready to take it on. Enjoy that hiatus because you deserve it. But as you see from my own experience, Old Fakey is no easy win, and he will creep in wherever he can. So you have to stay tuned for further instruction in every subsequent challenge.

That means if someone is telling you something you don't want to hear, that might be exactly the message you need to consider. It means you have to diligently and consistently recheck your attitude, perspective, perceptions, lies, and expectations, applying the APPLE Inventory to each specific situation. As I've learned along the way, you can commit it to memory, but you only get results by applying it. At any time you let this go and get lazy, you will know it because you will recognize the old funky thoughts creeping back in from their respective graves.

Just get yourself right back into the APPLE Inventory and move forward through the FRUITS Philosophy. You won't want to do it if you're already caught up. So decide today to commit to the process. Don't listen to the Fake-enlie that it is not working or things aren't changing. It took longer than a day to morph out of your True Self, and you will have to be determined to stick with it until you walk into the harvest you're cultivating. God will honor your commitment and let you know you're on the Path of Purpose and healing, even in the middle of the mess.

In the Middle of the Mess!

God can still bless you in the middle of whatever mess you find yourself. That is encouraging because it means, while we're blind and vulnerable, as long as He can get through to us, we make progress. The minute we divert from the path, we are back in the desert. I had Mosesitus for decades. By God's grace, I was still able to accomplish some things in that time. Stumbling around in that darkness, I fell into several divine opportunities that, in hindsight, were all part of the Master Plan.

Ever since dropping out of college, I had felt a profound urgency to go back to school. After almost twenty years of nightmares about getting to class late or missing a test, I finally enrolled. I had always been told I would be good at business, so I jumped at a new accelerated degree program in organizational leadership. That program ended the minute I graduated. That door opened and closed so fast any hesitation on my part would have ended with it slammed in my face. My nightmares ended with my first college degree. Again, just stumbling into things, that degree led to an ex-offender program that reflected the model suggested in my undergraduate thesis. I got to co-write the grant proposal. A graduate degree in social work followed, although I never had an aspiration for the profession, it is that training in psychotherapy and human behavior that positioned me to write this book. I fell into all of this by taking one obedient step at a time, as I understood God's leading— right in the middle of the mess.

One of my most remarkable opportunities came some years before college when, as a clueless, traumatized, twenty-two-year old, I landed in Chicago. I spent plenty of time in the hospital back then. Talk about a rotten mess. My life was drama's mama. I was homeless, living pillar to post. Although I was born there, I was new to the big city, having grown up in rural Hart, Michigan. I stuffed away a lot of grief because I had to keep pushing. My children were wards of the Detroit courts because I chose to marry some knucklehead, and I was running for my life without a penny in my pocket. Even in the middle of that mess, God was guiding my steps. The day I was discharged from one of my many hospital stays, my boyfriend, who played the trumpet, picked me up and took me straight to Universal Recording Studios. We walked in as Tyrone Davis was finishing lead vocals on "How Sweet it is to be Loved by You." Boy, it was sounding good. My boyfriend introduced me to the security guard with whom I remained friends even after we broke up.

After moving to Chicago's Gold Coast, I would drop into the studio from time to time. I had the run of the place and never thought a minute about wandering into Studio A one night. Quietly inviting myself in, I was mesmerized by the whole atmosphere. The music sounded so good. I decided to watch and see who was in charge. Noting a man to my right, I took the first opportunity to introduce myself. Extending a hand with my most professional demeanor, I said, "Hello, I'm Linda."

Quite graciously, and with a huge smile, he responded, "I'm Eugene Record."

What in the world is a Eugene Record? I hope my expression didn't reveal my confusion as I wondered, Is the guy for real? Record? Naw! Is he off or just that much into his profession? I shrugged it off and sat in the background. It took the next session for me to realize I was sitting in the presence of Eugene Record, the creative genius behind the doggone Chilites! Duh!

For the next four years, he and I wrote numerous songs, three of which they released. Even at that, it was another twenty-five years before I realized I was in the presence of music legends and pioneers of the Chicago music scene. These folks were to Chicago what Barry Gordy was to Motown!

WHOSE APPLE IS IT, ANYWAY!

One time I stepped into the Studio A lounge and there stood Smokey Robinson. At one of the Chilites' listening parties, I walked right into Jeffery Osborne. Seldom did a session exclude the likes of William "Sonny" Sanders, Thomas "Tom Tom 88" Washington. I was in the presence of giants such as James Mack, Leo Graham, Carl Davis, Gus Redmond, the Dells, all Chicago legends!

I still have the stub from my first royalty check after the Chilites released their *Bottoms Up* album. On side two sits my pride and joy, "You Take the Cake," which Eugene created from lyrics I wrote at my typewriter one day. Later came "Do What You Want" on the *Stepping Out* album and "Hard Act to Follow," which was released in the United Kingdom.

I always wanted to sing. I was in a gospel group in high school. But by the time I decided to work on my voice, the playback was atrocious! I started practicing for two or three hours several days a week using a tape recorder to practice with songs by Luther Vandross, Gladys Knight, and Peabo Bryson. Music was my life and I loved every moment of it. I was blindly functioning in my purpose and loving it. When I wasn't singing, I was writing or in the studio. Some nights I would be in the studio until two or three in the morning, grab some sleep, and go to my day job. All that ended when I married my second husband.

Destiny was redirected by marrying the wrong man. I got off the path, and it was costly. One day I was practicing at home when he came in and said, *"You sound like a man."* I was absolutely crushed. From that day on I sang less and less. Because I had internalized his criticism, that aspect of my talent went dormant. I have no idea why hearing it from him cut so deeply. I had heard it before. It was all par for the course, considering I couldn't write a bit of music the whole time I was married to this man. I tried and tried to no avail. Until very recently, the last note and lyric I wrote without forcing it was in June of 1985 when Eugene and I ended our writing partnership. I tried to go back to voice practice, but that lingering, nagging negativity ran through my every effort.

Years later, my mother and sisters called at various times to tell me I had to sing. My mother said that music is in me, and it is key to my purpose. They have told me and told me I have to push through this blockage. To date, that hasn't really happened. My speaking voice has a deep resonance, and I sing baritone and bass more comfortably than alto. The sound of my speaking, even in passing, causes strangers to stop and ask, "Do you sing? I know with a voice like that you must sing." I tell them "No, I don't" and laugh it off. Twenty years of creative lockdown in an area of your purpose is no laughing matter. I'm still healing from that wound, and I'm determined to sing again.

It's Up to You

Our life choices, our daily decisions can change the trajectory of our lives and short circuit God's plan. In every case, we are either the victim or the victor. The Hebrew crowd could have decided to listen to God. They chose, instead, to give into the fear of the past. Up to the border of the Promised Land Moses was able to call off judgment by praying to God on their behalf. The tenth time was the straw. Disqualified at point of entry! The entire nation suffered for it. It wasn't for lack of everything they needed to do the deal; it was due to stolen vision.

Before Moses was conceived, God established within him everything he needed to meet his date with destiny. He bestowed the same birthright on you, inclusive of all that lies beyond your Border of Destiny—your Promised Land. Look at that. Even though steeped in Egyptian culture, that God-inspired sense of calling, purpose, and destiny would not be denied. Remember, Moses was in the desert of Midian for forty years. How do you like that? Forty years of boot camp. It's a safe bet during that time, God dealt with him about a lot of things in preparation for the call. Those anger issues were likely a key aspect of His curriculum. But just as in the case of many men of God in Scripture, there was one thing in Moses' character that he wouldn't or couldn't relinquish.

Partial obedience is disobedience. Remember the classic scene where Moses struck the rock to get water instead of speaking to it as God had directed? That incident revealed a deeper condition of the heart that drove Moses' temper. It was his failure to overcome the issue that led to his being barred from the Promise Land. In the end, neither God's appointed Deliverer (Moses) nor His appointed priest (Aaron) would set foot in it. Aaron would never even see it. It was theirs all right; God gave it to them, and He never reneges. Only we can short circuit the plan. Destiny denied!

Our responses to life not only determine our future crops, but they affect others even when we are unaware. So when God insists on our obedience, it's not for His good, it's for the greater good. It's for the people whose lives will be, or are supposed to be, touched by ours. It's for the many whose blessings are to be channeled through us, for those whose freedom is tied to our obedience to God. Jesus got this. We grow up thinking He had some supernatural ability that we don't. That thinking contradicts Scripture (see Hebrews 4:15). He was all human and all God. We focus on the all-God part to the exclusion of the significance of the all-human part. Wow! What a massive sacrifice for God Himself to live in the confines of a human body, constricted and restricted. God is not subject to time and space. He went from being everywhere to the confines of fallible flesh that had to be fed, rested, washed, and repaired. That took a whole lot of love because Jesus was subject to the same human proclivities as we are. I wonder if we are missing the fact that even *His* human mind was not subject to God. It was against God, and it was incapable of understanding God. So all-God or not, He had His hands full keeping even His human mind in check. That battle was no more an easy win for Him than it is for us.

The power Jesus had is that He understood the mind is fair game, so he followed His Father's lead every step of the way. He moved and spoke on cue. It was a choice every time. That whole Garden of Gethsemane scene before the Crucifixion was no joke. He was struggling with His reasoning human mind, even to the point of telling God if there was any way out, He was up for it (see Luke 22:42). It took the entire God within Him to go through with it. From what I know of God, He left that decision up to His Son. His whole reason for going through that travesty, the very reason for His human existence, swung on that crucial moment. He was at His crossroads, and He had a decision to make. The Master Plan hung on His decision. Unlike Israel at their crossroads or Adam and Eve at theirs, Jesus did the right thing. In the grip of what must have been soul- rending fear, He did the right thing. What made the difference? Purpose!

Chapter 5: Date with Destiny

The Path of Purpose is paved with healing. At one end of that road is Destiny; at the other end is the town of Stolen Vision. They just renamed that town — it used to be called The Past. You have to know which way you're headed at every turn.

Every choice for purpose is a decision for destiny. Otherwise, you're heading the wrong way toward Stolen Vision. As you apply these strategies, you will notice your focus shifting. It feels as if it's turning you around. Don't be concerned — it won't turn you more than 180 degrees. It's realigning your direction with purpose as your perspective realigns with truth. There will be many battles along the way and many opportunities to use your skills. You are empowered by free will to fix each fight from the outset. Who wins is up to you. You're in control. It's a matter of choice; it's a matter of process.

Don't be Duped by the Fruit

Don't be duped by the fruit. Take it to the seed and you will always gain the understanding necessary for inside-out, deep-as-the-wound healing that ensures the self-awareness it takes to seed a better harvest. You have to examine your own motivations in order to gain a truer perspective of others' because it's at the seed that you root out Fake-enstein. Recognizing when behaviors are being driven by the past is germane to the process.

Sometimes those bogus apples get tossed, and sometimes they come at you at Bo Jackson speed! Consistently apply the APPLE Inventory and the FRUITS Philosophy, and you'll be ducking those suckers like Keanu Reeves in *The Matrix*![1]

So, when those emotions try to drive you where you don't want to go, remember the Garden Game. Say, *"This is not about me."* Take a deep breath and believe it, no matter how hard it is to do at the time. Find out what's behind it. As I said earlier, had Eve considered the serpent's motivations, she might have reaped a better outcome instead of trading her harvest (The Garden of Eden) for his (kicked off of the premises).

Going with Fake-enstein will always be about destroying purpose, vision, and destiny. It will never be about the Master Plan. It will never be about the greater good and that higher-than-the-game focus that, if maintained, will let you sidestep the mindfields laid to take you out of the game. That fruit will be tempting. At first, you will find it easier to take a bite than to resist. But if you examine it at its core, examining the seeds, and acting accordingly, you will surely gain the understanding that takes you outside your own agenda and into destiny.

At the Core

At the seed you'll find the backstory, the motivations behind your own responses. You can't fake the fruit for long before Old Fakey has to make himself known. As you progress in your self-discernment, it will be easier to spot relationships that are going nowhere and act accordingly. It's important to know when to cut your losses and move on. There is no room on Purpose Road for dead weight, so don't let folks crowd you off the path.

I know of a woman who was in a committed relationship with a man who treated her very well at first. He bought her a fine car and took her places she had never been. She thought she had finally found true love. Initially, when they had disagreements it was difficult, but they successfully worked through the rough spots. When he suddenly put his own vanity plates on the car he gave her, she had a clue something was wrong. She had asked him to put her initials on it, but he was headstrong on having it his way. She figured out the car was just a grandiose overture to make him look like the big savior. He never really gave the car to her; it was his all along.

Another "red flag" incident she could not ignore was the time she was bleeding from an apparent urinary tract infection. She was in no shape to make the trip to the drug store without multiple bathroom stops along the way. This man stood there looking at the blood, refused to go pick up the prescription, and then went back to watching his ball game. She went to get her own medications. He never showed a bit of remorse or regret. Nor did he offer any indication that what he did was wrong. Meanwhile he ran out of town when his sister had hand surgery, and when his daughter had her gall bladder removed, he was all over social media asking for prayers. He was incapable of seeing his own wrong. That's how entrenched Fake-enstein was in him. The man shut down, refused to hear any truth, and the relationship deteriorated into a no-affection, no-communication series of bouts with his withdrawal and passive aggressive behaviors.

This woman was confused. What she once affectionately called his Mean-Ole-Man personality was starkly opposite of the man she loved. She actually identified three different personalities in this one man:

Personality A adored her, hands-in-pockets, looking like an innocent little boy. That little boy threw tantrums when he didn't get his way. *Personality B* was even-keel and well adjusted, easy to talk to, affectionate, and loving. *Personality C* was the backside of B — the controlling, fixated man with no empathy for anybody. He crumbled like a cracker under pressure. His mantra was, *"I'm thinking about me right now."*

The dichotomy was confusing and frightening as she saw less of the nice guy and more of the bad personality. She supported the man through two years of unemployment while being told to "stay out of his business," and putting up with verbal and emotional abuse. He even had the nerve mid-argument to ask her, "*Who supported you when I first came here?*" He was unemployed when they met and only worked a total of eight to nine months during their almost three-year relationship.

One day she was sitting at her computer when the word narcissism came to mind. She looked it up. It was him! What a forehead slapper. He met all diagnostic criteria for narcissistic personality disorder. From the inability to make a decision and stick with it to the lack of empathy or concern for others, he was a textbook example of the disorder. He had difficulty regulating his emotions, had a history of multiple failed interpersonal relationships on all levels, showed classic signs of a sense of entitlement, and suffered repeated delusions of grandeur. The man was so deluded he kept talking about writing an autobiography that nobody in the world would care to read because nobody knew this man from Adam's housecat. This woman had multiple warning signs along the way. Her Fake-enstein kept her from cutting her losses. The healing that leads to controlling our own Fake-enstein empowers us to see clearly, set appropriate boundaries with others, and set immutable boundaries with ourselves. We discern when to disengage from negativity as opposed to going along for the useless ride. As we heal, we see truth, we develop keen discernment and we sidestep destiny- destroying mindfields before they wreak destruction in our lives. Healing is empowering. It strategically positions us on the playing field. From this position of strength, from this strategic vantage point, we find Fakey before he finds us!

Fakey Hates Change

Every victory strengthens you for the next battle. You'll want to remember that because you will need it. It takes a determined focus to win fights with Old Fakey. Change is his demise, and he knows it. The change you want to see should be your focus, not the battle. Remember the cosmic chess game we talked about in the early part of the book? God has His plan for you, but you get to choose whether to cooperate with it. That is a battle of mind against your will. That battle takes focus and consistent application of the APPLE Inventory and the FRUITS

Philosophy. In consistency lies the power. To effect change you will have to keep your vision forward (toward purpose and destiny), maintain an unrelenting focus on being the change you want to *see*, obey God, and consistently apply the battle plan.

When under fire obedience is your counterattack. Mosesitus blinds you to divine opportunities and connections. Be determined to ignore Fakey-Jake and hear, accept, heed, and follow through on all good counsel and God's direction. That way you won't miss these opportunities, even if you're still not seeing clearly. You have to trust the process because your focus has been off for so long. You've been too long in the dark.

Your True Self is an emerging work in progress. It will take a minute for your spiritual eyes to adjust to the light. You will need guidance and support along the way. Listen to wise counsel and act accordingly. These are people God placed on the path to guide, protect, or help you at times when you're blinded to your own vulnerabilities. If your focus is off, you might miss destiny because, even with a solid focus, it might not look as you expect.

Destiny doesn't always arrive in a pretty package. It can look strange and foreign, nothing like anything you would have imagined; that is, if you've ever thought about it at all. That's because you have been somebody else for so long. It will seem strange at first as you become oriented along your Path of Purpose.

Playing to a Purpose Higher than the Game

Truth is new to you on this path of healing. It's foreign and doesn't feel right because Fake-enstein's still fighting for his life. Don't go with Fakey. Don't listen to him. Don't even think about it. Instead, shut up, suck it up, and listen up. Repeat that phrase to yourself when those emotions rise up, "Shut up, suck it up, and listen up." Resist the natural urge to lash out, refuse to listen, talk over the speaker, or argue. Whatever way your Fake-enstein acts out— don't do it. The temptation will be strong to fight against any truth or correction, so decide right now not to go there. Get busy with the APPLE Inventory and back up long enough to pull your True Self together. Start ignoring Old Fakey. Recognize it as the distraction it is and move forward to your game plan. You've spent enough time being him.

You never know when a missed opportunity might be your last chance to get it right. This is a time for unrelenting focus. Don't take your eyes off the vision. You have to focus hard now because looking away for a second diverts focus. Stolen focus means stolen vision. Stolen vision means stolen destiny. At every opportunity, remind yourself of that. When you have never caught the vision, you might not recognize its arrival. So when it gets tough, remember to always play to a purpose higher than whatever mind game Old Fakey's playing.

Playing to a Purpose Higher than the Game

Former New England Patriots player, Curtis Martin, led the American Football Conference (AFC) in rushing *as a rookie*. He was the second player in National Football League (NFL) history to start a career with ten straight one-thousand-yard rushing seasons.[2] He moved on to lead his team in rushing every season, with a career high of 1,697 yards. He ended his stellar career as the fourth all-time leading rusher in NFL history, racking up 14,101 yards. The man scored 100 rushing and receiving touchdowns for combined net yards of 17,421.

On August 4, 2012, Curtis Martin was inducted into the NFL Hall of Fame, never having been a fan of the game! That's right, he was never a fan of the game, and he accomplished all this without ever fully understanding what he called the "X's and O's of football."[3] And, get this, the man absolutely *hated* to run.

Okay, hold the phone. What? He must have been playing with more passion than he's letting on because he was *good*. He made it into the Hall of Fame without even *caring* about the game? Yes, without even the slightest love for the game, something drove him *hard*.

The Backstory

Curtis's father used to torture his mother by making her sit in a tub of hot water. Every time she flinched, he would burn her with cigarettes or take a lighter to her hair. Five-year-old Curtis saw it happen:

> *I've seen him beat her up like she was a man. I've seen him throw her down the steps. I've witnessed this woman, my mother, get punched in the face, have a black eye, and then*

go to work with make up on just to support our family.[4]

Curtis spoke of his mother's taking three jobs after his father left. As early as kindergarten, he was often left home alone until his mother came home from work. It broke his mother's heart every time she took those stairs at night. She could see her baby-sitting in the window as she crossed the street. She knew he was scared.

At nine years old, Curtis remembered his mom finding her mother stabbed to death in her bed: a knife in her chest, neck broken, eyes wide open. That's gruesome, but real. He never said he was with her at the time, but his vivid description sounds like a firsthand account. That's way too much trauma for any adult to endure, much less a child.

And for me as a little kid, all the other family, they come in and you hear the whispers from adults as a little kid, and they affect you a certain way. I just heard everyone saying, "If that happened to me, I would go crazy. I would lose my mind." For me, crazy was kind of like what my dad was. So in my mind, as a nine-year-old, my mother told me the only thing that got her through that was I came up to her and grabbed her hand and said, "Mom, are you going crazy?" And she looked down at me and said, "No. Why do you ask me that?" And I just said, "Well, that's good because if you go crazy, nobody's going to be here to take care of me."[5]

At age thirteen, Curtis' aunt "died an even worse or more painful death" than his grandmother. Fear and danger were daily realities for this child:

I had so many brushes with death. I remember . . . a guy had a gun to my head, a loaded gun to my head, pulled the trigger seven times. God's honest truth, the bullet didn't come out. He wasn't pointing the gun at me and pulled the trigger and a bullet came out. I was too young to even recognize that God was saving my life.[6]

Curtis was convinced he wouldn't live to age twenty-one. After trauma every four years since the age of five, he was probably right. Caught up in the street life and hopeless, he had no upbringing to include God. But some how he knew that God was his last possible option. He brought it straight from the heart the best he knew how:

I said, "Listen, man, I don't know nothing about you or this Jesus cat that everybody talks about, but I'm going to make a deal with you. I heard about people making deals with the devil, but I don't want to do that. I'm going to make a deal with you. If you let me live past 21, dude, I promise that I'll just try to do my best and try to live right and try to do whatever you want me to do. I know you're a smart person, if you're God. So there has to be a bigger purpose for my life than what I'm experiencing. There's got to be more to life than this."[7]

Note that even in this mess and against all odds, Curtis had a sense of both purpose and of his Creator.

I tell you what. I'm thirty-nine years old now, and God has definitely upheld His end of the bargain, and I'm going to spend the rest of my life trying to do mine, uphold my end of the bargain.[8]

And that he did. Let's take a look at some of the divine connections Curtis encountered and examine the destiny decisions he made along the way.

Crossroads

When Curtis got the call from Bill Parcells inviting him to play for the Patriots, he accepted, hung up, turned around to his family and said:

"Oh my gosh, I do not want to play football. I don't want to play football. I don't even know that I like football enough to try to make a career out of it."[9]

As you read through this story, a pattern of divine connections emerges. God placed certain people around this young man, people Curtis could have easily overlooked. His pastor was one. Had it not been for Curtis's fateful deal with God, his pastor wouldn't likely have been a part of his life at all. The pastor said, *"Curtis, look at it this way, man. Maybe football is just something God is giving you so you can do all those wonderful things that you say you want to do for other people."*[10]

Did you notice the pastor's reference to purpose? For Curtis it struck a spiritual nerve. Also, note the man's heart in this. He wanted to help others; his focus wasn't driven by money, fame, or fortune. It was all about what he could do for somebody else.

I tell you, it was like a light bulb came on in my head. And

> *ever since he said that, I knew the only way I was going to be successful at football is if I played for a purpose that was bigger than the game itself because I knew that the love for the game just wasn't in my heart.*[11]

Curtis took wise advice at his crossroads because he tapped into his purpose instead of lack of motivation for the game. That was the second step of obedience. The first step of obedience came when, seeing her son's direction, Curtis's mother insisted he find something to do for two hours after school each day. At the urging of his high school coach, he took up high school football. That high school coach was a divine connection and a step along the Path of Purpose that lead to Coach Parcell's offer.

I was struck by an interview with this young man. I'd never heard of him before then. Yet, by the time it was over, I was a lifetime fan. The interviewer asked Curtis how he could rack up a Hall of Fame performance given his lack of interest in the game. His answer was beyond profound: "I guess I was playing to a purpose higher than the game."[12] What led this man to stardom was his vision to help other people, not the least of which was his mother. He had a higher purpose.

> *My greatest achievement in my life was helping my mother and nurturing [her] from the bitter, angry, beaten, hurt person that she was, nurturing her to be . . . healthy, to have a healthy mindset, and to forgive my father for everything that he did to her. That's my greatest accomplishment.*[13]

Mission accomplished. Mission successful and his mother met her Promised Land through him. His father passed away knowing she forgave him because she was there for him in his last days.

> *By the time he died, she was cooking him food every day and taking it to him. And she is so happy right now, and I'm so grateful for her.*[14]

Because, as a teenager, Curtis was obedient to authority, he found a higher purpose (providing for his mother), he played the game he didn't love with excellence, and God honored that obedience to the end. There's nothing in Curtis's background to set him up for this kind of obedience. It was his love for his mother and the honor and respect it entailed that drove him through the running he hated, the Xs and Os that challenged him, and a horrible childhood that few could have survived. At his crossroads, Curtis made the right decision. It made the difference in his life, and it was the link to his mother's happiness. Absent his obedience, the family curse so evident in his story would have never been broken.

By his obedience, he drew the blood of Jesus across that mess and left a positive legacy for future generations. Had he been on Mosesitus lockdown, he wouldn't have listened to the divine connections God orchestrated to guide him out of multigenerational darkness. He summed it up this way:

> Out of all the things I've achieved, it's not necessarily what you achieve in life that matters most, but it's who you become in the process of those achievements that really matters.[15]

Curtis found his True Self through one-step-at-a-time obedience and acting on guidance from the connections God orchestrated in his life.

> At my eulogy, I don't want my daughter . . . to talk about how many yards I gained or touchdowns I scored. I want my daughter to be able to talk about the man Curtis Martin was. How when she was growing up, she looked for a man who was like her father. That he was a man of integrity, a man of strong character, and a God-fearing man. That's what I want. Then at the end of the day, she could say, "Oh yeah, and he was a pretty good football player."[16]

Curtis has it right. He found his Path of Purpose, and it didn't look anything like what he could have imagined. He was offered a challenge he says his heart wasn't in. He took it on with unyielding focus and vision. He listened to the people God provided to guide him. He didn't question whether he could do it. He went at it as if his life depended on it without realizing how true that was. In the final analysis his life, his mother's life, and anybody else's life connected with him, *depended* on those decisions.

What stood between Curtis and his destiny was a series of choices made at various crossroads in his life. At every crossroad, there was a divine connection to facilitate his purpose. Right in the middle of chaos he saw it, he listened, and he took good and wise advice. It made the difference between destruction and destiny for so many. He had that all-important higher focus. Life dealt him a sorry hand, but he leveraged what he had, mixed in focus and a determined goal, and out of it, he got much more than he had imagined possible. That harvest is eternal. It will perpetuate well after he's gone. He leveraged adversity and made it count!

Make it Count

I once worked across the hall from a woman who lived in constant fear of something happening to her daughter. She was crazy about the girl and poured herself into her daughter lock, stock, and barrel. Within a year or so of meeting this woman, her daughter was killed in a personal watercraft accident, the circumstances of which are still quite cloudy. The loss took the worst toll on this woman, and she was filled with grief and confusion. She would talk about it with such heaviness that it was almost palpable.

One day, feeling her frustration, I decided to walk her through thinking about the things that mattered to her daughter. I thought it might facilitate her healing and redirect her focus from what she could do nothing to change. As she told me about her daughter, an intermittent smile appeared, and I could sense a healthy defiance rising up in her. Going with that flow and with every bit of the same power she was beginning to realize, I said, "You make it count!" She lit up and told me later what a difference it made for her. She was on her way out of the bondage of victimization to power and victory.

At the point of infliction, we often become victims. Whether we remain victims is a matter of choice. Getting stuck there instead of going on through the healing process keeps us stuck at that point on the Master Plan timeline, short circuiting destiny.

Becoming the *victor* depends on our determination to *make it count*. That's the only revenge we're allowed. We can decide the pain and trauma will not win by leveraging it toward a higher purpose. That's not going to happen as long as we remain mired in bitterness, lack of forgiveness, anger, fear, retaliation, denial, or revenge. You might very well have a reason to feel all of those things, but the blood and cross of Jesus say you have no right! God has our backs with respect to vengeance against the offenders, and He alone holds the power and right to judge. We leverage it by remembering that in every challenge lies opportunity. We leverage it by making it count.

What God did for Curtis, He's done for you. Even in the middle of a mess, God is orchestrating destiny around you. You could be walking by it every day. Just as He did for Curtis, He's doing all He can to orchestrate your best shot at destiny. Wait! Look over there! Destiny awaits you. So what are you waiting for? Go for it!

Plain Talk: Terminology

Because these principles are the foundation of this journey, I'm giving you what I call a Christianese translation of spiritual terms and phrases that undergird the concepts of this book.

Christian Terminology

Here's a breakdown of some Christian terms you have encountered on this journey. You have likely heard some of these before. I thought it helpful to discuss them as they relate to the context of the book.

Have the Mind of Christ

The human mind is God's natural enemy (see Roman 8:7). Plain and simple, it is enemy territory, so don't fool yourself. It neither conceives nor perceives of purpose, mission, or destiny because these are spiritual matters. The mind isn't even subject to God's law, so it's up to us to handle our own business in this regard. The only way to do this is through our spirit, which is the part of us that connects with God. It will take God's direction (spiritual discernment) to navigate the pitfalls into which our minds trick us. Once we get our thinking in line with truth, we're considered to have the mind of Christ.

Warning: when perfection becomes the goal, we are automatically enslaved to guilt and disappointment for never achieving some unrealistic man-concocted nirvana set up as a pseudo-measure of faith or commitment to God. So, if perfection is the focus, *news flash*: if you have a belly button, you're a sinner, buddy! Your record is already ruined. If you're human with a heartbeat, you've already made mistakes. Accept it. Moving on … Now that's established, answer this question: everybody's *talking* about this spiritual nirvana, but who has ever made the grade in that respect?

Being human was no easy win for Jesus either. Check Him out in the Garden of Gethsemane before His execution. Even this man, who was *all* God and *all* man, had to deal with His humanity. Trust me. Being human was no cakewalk for Him, either. Just because He's the Son of God didn't mean His humanity was an easy win. He walked in the same human flesh with which we struggle. He had no more power over his human mind than we do. There is no mystery — just reality. It took an act of His will. He had to make moment-by-moment decisions to handle His business where His human mind was concerned.

How Jesus did it is no mystery either. He knew His human mind was not going along with the spiritual game plan. He kept it in check by saying what God told Him to say or do, when He was told to say or do it. He did it one-step, one day at a time, one foot in front of the other. In other words, it's a *process* that involves leveraging your will. Step one in that process is recognizing and accepting that as long as they are not subject to God, our minds are extremely vulnerable. Step two is being open to the change it takes to control the mind, as opposed to the mind controlling you.

In the Flesh (Carnal)

The word carnal has gotten a bad rap in Christian circles. When we're acting out, we're told that we're *in the flesh*. We're told to stop being *carnal*. It's a catchall phrase for sin. Who knows what it really means to be in the flesh, let alone how to fix it? While the Bible clearly says not to be "carnally minded," I didn't understand how that looked in real life. The Bible says, "Because the carnal mind is enmity against God: for it is not subject to the law of God, neither indeed can be" (Romans 8:7). I went to the root of the Greek word to learn its intended meaning:

- Exposed flesh (after pulling back the skin)
- Road kill (animal carcass)
- The human body
- Human nature (with its frailties physical, moral, or emotional)
- Human being (as such carnally minded). A symbol for the external as opposed to the spiritual.[1]

We're not skinning anybody here, and I don't think any of us are road kill, so for purposes of this discussion, *carnal* means "human nature with its frailties physical, moral, or emotional." It basically means being a meathead- spiritually numb from the neck up. This verse shows that we cannot relate to God out of our intellect or human thinking (being a meathead). We can only relate to God through our spirits. This is the reason we always want our souls to gravitate toward our spirits, because, through the spirit, we have relationship with God. It's through that dynamic phenomenon that we find the strength and guidance to change from thinking our *own* way, to thinking a new way.

Someone is considered "in the flesh" (see Isaiah 55:8–9) when they are reacting out of negative emotions. This isn't about the physical body as much as it is about the mind. When emotions take over, our response to an event can be way over the top. It's usually a sign that some part of our defense system (defined below) has been challenged as we respond to a *perceived*, often nonexistent, threat. Let's call it being *stuck on stupid* because when it happens, we're emotionally hijacked by the past, and we act as if we're right back where the hurt first happened. On a subconscious level, we're stuck, and our responses and behaviors are inappropriate to the situation or the circumstance at hand.

Harvest

Thoughts are seeds that produce an outcome. That outcome is called a harvest. These seeds produce (reap) after their own kind, resulting in either a good or bad crop (harvest) depending on what behavior results. If our thinking doesn't line up with reality or truth, it can lead to bad choices. This reap-what- you-sow principle applies to every aspect of our lives. Remember, though, your harvest is based *only* on what *you* do, not what others do to you. You'll understand this better further on in the text.

Know Who You Are in Christ (True Self)

I call this your True Self, who God saw when He planned your existence (see Jeremiah 1:5). Before you or your parents were born (1 Peter 1:2), He knew and created you for destiny and purpose. Your calling was established at that time, and what He says goes, without exception. Things get off track, though, when life experiences mutate our True Selves into complete opposites. Because we have to be our True Selves to accomplish our individual callings and missions, this mutation is destiny-lethal.

No matter how we get twisted and disjointed by life experiences, He sees us as He made us. Case closed where He's concerned. The disconnection between how we see ourselves and how God sees us is ground navigated in these pages. You're holding the roadmap back to your True Self, and the game plan that propels you along your Path of Purpose.

Master Plan

This is the game plan, the cosmic blueprint, the intricate and complicated universal strategy for accomplishing God's creative purpose. It encompasses multiple dimensions and transcends time. Because it is executed *through us*, getting things accomplished is complicated by our own free wills. Whether we get with the program or not determines how well we, and others who are divinely connected to us, fare in the final outcome.

Path of Purpose

It's unfortunate that it has taken near-death experiences for some people to recognize that they are here for a reason. The truth is that everybody's here for a reason, and enemy strategy involves keeping us off that focus at every available opportunity. When we're distracted by things unrelated to purpose, we're off course and headed down the wrong path. There are only two ways to go — *toward* or *away* from destiny. You are either on the Path of Purpose or on a path to disappointment and destruction.

Individuals have unique paths to travel in order to reach their own God-intended destinies. As we move through life, situations and circumstances can knock us off that path. As we internalize painful experiences, we lose the ability to see truth. Each time something blindsides us, we get up and step it off, never recognizing that we're off track. Some of our experiences are so devastating they change the entire trajectory of our lives. When we don't take time to process that pain and regain our bearings, we keep walking but in the wrong direction.

God's Truth is the compass that keeps us on the Path of Purpose. Twisted perceptions ensure that we never see our True Selves. Your True Self is part of the tool kit, specially designed to facilitate your specific purpose in the Master Plan. This tool kit contains everything you need to execute any assigned missions along the way. When thoughts are aligned with truth, God directs our path, and purpose is revealed and accomplished with each step we take along that path. Everything you need, every person for whom you are a divine connection, and every person who is a divine connection for you, is along your own Path of Purpose.

This Path of Purpose is paved with inside-out healing. Getting realigned along that path involves a process of self-reflection, self-realization, and submission to what God reveals along the way. It's going to take a new kind of focus, no matter what; to gain the skill it takes to *stay* in your lane!

Calling Versus Mission

A mission is a task or duty. It's defined by Miriam Webster as "a task or job that someone is given to do." It is closely related to vocation, which is described as a "Strong inclination to a particular state or course of action" or "the special function of an individual or group."[1] In spiritual context, a mission can be the responsibility of multiple players. You may not see or know all the players in a Master Plan mission. As the commander-in-chief, *God* knows. Following the commander's direction is germane to a successfully executed mission.

Within each mission, there are a series of assignments. For example, at any given time, if we're discerning, we might get an urge to go see this person or pay for that person's groceries, or stop and talk to a stranger. The list is endless. The mission is accomplished one-step at a time as we follow through with each assignment.

According to Webster's, *calling* is "a strong desire to spend your life doing a certain kind of work" or "the work that a person does or should be doing."[2] This is related to your specific part in the overall mission. If you are a naturally talented writer, you might be called to that vocation. If you have a beautiful singing voice, you might be called to sing. If you are a naturally good communicator, or if you naturally encourage others, those, too, might be your callings.

To find your calling, think about whatever irks you. Is there a particular social injustice that gets you going? It might reveal a clue to your calling. Also, ask yourself what it is you love to do. Do you love sculpting, painting, music? Are you a natural communicator, a peacemaker? Do you have any natural personality characteristics that make you a good lawyer, social worker, or teacher? The answers to those questions hold clues to what you are called to do.

Successfully executing your calling requires knowing and utilizing all the tools in your tool kit. This tool kit contains your natural talents, and abilities. This is what the enemy is after — your tool kit. Why? It's because your tool kit *also* contains your personality and character. Every other tool in that kit is strong and unrelentingly effective as long as your personality and character are intact. If they are not, the tools lose some or all of their power.

You must become who God created you to be (True Self) for these tools to operate at full power. So it's an effective enemy strategy to target our personalities and characters. He doesn't have to worry about our other tools as long as he can effectively morph us out of our True Selves. He knows that locking us down there will render the rest of the tools ineffective.

So, you are called to a purpose. To accomplish that purpose requires a successfully accomplished mission that involves numerous assignments along the way. It's kind of a military setup. If you skip an assignment, the overall mission could fail, and everybody else involved in that mission could suffer setbacks. So think about a mission as involving various players all working in harmony with the Master Plan.

Nobody's mission gets accomplished in a chasm. Our lives are interrelated that way. Therefore, nobody's mission is effectively accomplished unless everyone involved focuses on their individual assignments. If somebody drops the ball, the Master Plan does not change. The strategy, however, suffers and getting there becomes more complicated for us. If God has to use someone else to get the deal done, I'm sure He will. But I don't want to have to face the end of the war having to explain why I refused to get with the program.

Faith without Works

Taking God at His word and acting accordingly summarizes the faith-works connection. *Faith* is just a word without the backup. Without action behind it, it's dead on arrival (DOA). That's where works come into play. There's no use sitting around believing something without *acting* on it. If you believe you can go back to school and earn a degree, for instance, but never lift a finger to enroll, it's all for naught. Degrees aren't conferred based on how hard a person believes it; they are conferred for well-earned hard work! You act on what God says, even though it's uncomfortable and the complete opposite of what you're used to even when you don't auto-*magically* see results.

Nothing worth having is ever an easy win. After years of wrong-way momentum, it will feel as if you are trudging through mud at first. So, in the interest of taking God at His word, it will take believing a lot of what you're not used to before your head finally announces the change to your heart. When that happens, it's a supernatural moment that triggers the universe to get with the program. It's all over but the shouting from there!

Sadly, most of us have been doing this in reverse. So, it's not the principle of "faith meets works" that causes us challenges. It's all that force behind the *wrong* thinking that's got us running rogue. I suggest a *fake-it-till-you-make-it* approach. The work that gives life to faith happens when you keep doing it because God said so. When you do it because of who *He* is, then it's no longer about *you*; it's about calling, mission, purpose, and destiny. It's about *your* part in the Master Plan.

Plain Talk: General Terminology

Here's a breakdown of some non-Christian terms you will encounter on this journey. You have likely heard some of these. I thought it helpful to discuss them as they relate to the context of the book.

Attitude

When you think of *attitude*, think of *altitude*. Our thought lives drive our attitudes. Our attitudes will take us to higher heights with respect to purpose and destiny, or they will keep us from reaching those heights. Attitude consists of a combination of our perceptions and perspectives. Our *perceptions* (how we experience the world around us) inform our *perspectives* (conclusions we draw from how we experience the world around us). Based on that, we ascribe to a set of expectations of others. Those expectations, whether conscious or subconscious, will bring us exactly what we expect. If grounded in lies from the past, they bring more of the pain that caused us to believe those lies. If they are grounded in the truth, our expectations will align with our God-ordained destinies.

Attitude is born out of our overall life experiences, and it is colored by how we coped, or failed to cope, with past trauma, adversity, or painful life experiences. It embodies all the reasons we see the glass as half-empty or full. We'll be discussing this dynamic more later.

Defense System

This is a habitual, knee-jerk, reaction from some past event that causes us to think we have to protect ourselves from ever going there again. It hardens us to change while at the same time fooling us into reacting to perceived threats (often lies), none of which are based in truth or reality. The pervasive problem here is that we're then walking around exuding expectations of more of the same negativity. That's the seed we constantly plant, and that's the crop we consistently yield.

Denial

This is the refusal to accept or deal with current or past reality. Denial, properly placed, helps us get through trauma and stress.[2] But "*getting* through" and "*moving* through" are two different things. If denial goes too long, it's out of balance. By then it's time-out for just getting through the trauma. At some point, we have to move through denial to acceptance. Absent that, true healing is impossible.

Frame of Reference

Your Frame of Reference is how you see or interpret the world around you -- your worldview, your take on things, your point of view, and it's all driven by your life experiences, good and bad. How you make decisions is fully influenced on all possible levels by your Frame of Reference. Opinions and decisions swing on how you see the world around you. Rule one is accepting that just because something makes perfect sense to you doesn't mean it lines up with reality or truth.

The Defense System comes into play here. As long as you are reacting out of past trauma or negative life experiences, you are living in that past drama and reacting to here-and-now events based on lies perpetuated by the Defense System. This builds up scars around your heart. It's important to note here that this system of lies is designed to keep the defenses in existence. The systemic spiritual poisoning it perpetuates is meant to keep it alive. Self-survival, at any cost, is at the core of the Defense System's modus operandi. We will talk more on this in detail later. Right now, just remember that distorting our frames of reference is job one of the defensive strategy.

Personal Responsibility

Own it! I call this personal *respond*-ability because it involves owning our own parts in creating the realities we live. Even in the middle of situations or circumstances outside our control, our personal harvest is determined by how we respond smack-dab in the middle of whatever mess comes along. For example, if somebody approaches you wrongly about a matter, it's not all right to shoot back the same venom she threw your way. In that moment personal responsibility means you control impulse and deliberately choose a different response.

In that moment, it's not about how wrong she was. That's *her* harvest to cultivate or weed out as she sees fit. Your responses seed your future harvest. That means you get past how she brought it wrong and determine if there is any truth in the message. If there is, take responsibility for the change it takes to address it. You might find out it's you who owes the apology and not your friend.

Mindfields

The entire Defense System sets up enemy ground. Any defensive thoughts are almost always based on irrational and unrealistic lies we've told ourselves about, and as a result of, past trauma or painful life experiences. These lies lurk out of conscious sight. We don't see them, even as they insidiously rule our lives. These areas are referred to as enemy *mind*fields. Just as minefields in war are planted with explosive devices, so mindfields are replete with destiny- destroying landmines. One false move and you're caught up in an irrational emotional discharge (IED).

Irrational Emotional Discharges

If you step on a landmine, it explodes on contact. They are hidden for that very purpose. If you see it first, you won't detonate it. Similarly, an Irrational Emotional Discharge (IED) occurs whenever the Defense System hijacks our emotions. Giving in to this dynamic leaves destruction in its wake.

Whether IEDs are manifest internally or externally, they are always based on lies that to us seem well justified. The destruction can be in the form of repeated relationship drama, arguments, isolation, jealousy, bitterness, lack of forgiveness, anger, or hurt feelings. How IEDs manifest in your life wholly depends on the design of your specific Defense System.

For some it rears up as a fear of speaking up for themselves. For others it's speaking up too much or at the wrong time. In yet another case, it results in the wrong or inappropriate behavior. Some people withdraw into themselves, isolate, or ruin any relationship that gets too close. It often comes in the form of offense. For example, we get offended at someone's treatment of us, how a person talked to us. We become offended at something they did, how they dress, or how they carry themselves. It can be an angry outburst that you think was justified. It can come in the form of being overly sensitive. However, an IED manifests, rest assured you will never see it coming before it explodes. Unless you leverage the tools to root them out, they will hijack your entire existence.

Mosesitus

This is another word for the mindsets that keep us stuck in the past. It encompasses the denial that feeds the Defense System. Denial courses through the veins of this system because without it, the Defense System could not survive. It is later referred to as a *total eclipse of the mind*.

Fake-enstein

Fake-enstein is another name for the Defense System. Just as Frankenstein is made up of a conglomerate of dead bodies, so are our defenses made up of negativity from the past. As we internalize wrongs, they become part of us and morph us out of our True Selves. By internalizing (brooding, harboring anger, lack of forgiveness) trauma, pain, or the wrongs we endure, we *become* the wrong that was *done* to us. This causes us to react to every subsequent situation or circumstance as if we were still in the past. We talk more about this analogy in the "Living in the Past" section.

You will see Fake-enstein referred to as Old Fakey and Fakey-Jake, or Fakey as we reveal the Fake-enlies he constantly tells us. Now that we're on the same page term-wise, let's lay a bit of groundwork with some basic, yet unyielding, universal truths.

Notes

Preface

1. Raising a Sensory Smart Child: the Definitive Handbook for Helping Your Child, Nancy Peske (Penguin Books: New York, NY 2009).

Introduction

1. Meyer, J. (2011). Battlefield of the mind: Winning the battle in your mind. New York: FaithWords.

2. Warren, R. (2002). The purpose-driven life: What on earth am I here for? Grand Rapids, Michigan: Zondervan.

Plain Talk: Christian Terminology

1. Merriam Webster® Unabridged Dictionary Fourth Edition (Miriam Webster: Springfield, MA 2006).
2. Strong, J. The New Strong's Concordance of the Bible (Thomas Nelson, Inc.: Nashville, TN 1996).
3. [Ibid]

Chapter 1

1. Merriam Webster® Unabridged Dictionary Fourth Edition (Miriam Webster: Springfield, MA 2006).

2. Catherine Austin Fitts (2008). In Ruppert, Michael C. The Truth and Lies of 9/11. From the Wilderness Publications. [Video]: www.fromthewilderness. com Retrieved from http://www.youtube.com/watch?v=lqM90eQi5-M

Chapter 3

1. Hauser, K. (2009). How to Graft Your Own Apple Orchard (p.1). Riverside, CA: Kuffel Creek Press. Retrieved September 16, 2012, fromhttp://www.uffelcreek.com/GrowingApples/GraftAppleOrchard.pdf

1. Kline, A. S. (2002). Virgil: The Aeneid Book VIII Translation by A. S. Kline.
2. Ramis, H. (Director). (1993). Groundhog day [Film]. Columbia Tristar Films.
3. "Strengthening Your Grip on Attitudes," Swindoll, Charles R. (Charles R. Swindoll, Incorporated 1981).

4. Ibid.

5. Ibid.

6. The American Heritage® Dictionary of the English Language, Fourth Edition (Houghton Mifflin Company: Boston, MA 2000).

    1. Collins Thesaurus of the English Language, 2nd Edition. (HarperCollins Publishers: New York, NY 1995, 2002).

2. "Strengthening Your Grip on Attitudes," Swindoll, Charles R. (Charles R. Swindoll, Incorporated 1981).

3. Ibid.

4. Ibid.

5. Ibid.

6. Ibid.

7. Ibid

8. "Immaculée Ilibagiza," K. Winston (2006). Beliefnet. Para. 4. Retrieved on August 23, 2008 from: http://www.beliefnet.com/story/203/story_20381_...

    Chapter 5

1. Matrix, The. Dir. Andy Wachowski and Larry Wachowski. (Warner Bros. Pictures, 1999).

Chapter 6
1. Curtis Martin Jr. NFL Hall of Fame Induction Speech, Canton, Ohio(August 2012). Retrieved on December 26, 2012, from the National Football League Hall of Fame website http://www.cantonrep.com/sports/hall_of_ fame/x5...
2. Ibid.
3. Ibid.
4. Ibid.
5. Ibid.
6. Ibid.
7. Ibid.
8. Ibid.
9. Ibid.
10. Ibid.
11. Ibid.
12. Ibid.
13. Ibid.
14. Ibid.

About the Author

For Linda, a profound result of writing Whose Apple is it Anyway! was seven years of shedding layers of trauma, disappointment, and one bad destiny-diverting heartbreak after another. But, every layer shed brought clarity of vision as she has turned that pain into purpose – helping others find their purpose and leverage their past to empower destiny.

Linda is a survivor of rape, domestic violence, homelessness, and a 17-year marriage to a man later convicted as a rapist. She has the insight to recognize how emotional trauma and painful experiences lead to self-defeating behaviors that shout down purpose and immobilize destiny. She knows, from experience, the courage it takes to face down the past; and she is living proof that, "A lifetime of change is empowered by a single act of courage."

As the founder of Whose Apple Dynamic Coaching and Consulting Services, she is the creator of The Whose Apple Dynamic® GPS 360 Success Map™. Linda is a Certified Personal and Professional Life Coach, behaviorist, and trained psychotherapist, and motivational speaker.

Whose Apple Dynamic Coaching and Consulting Services

Your Personal and Professional Empowerment Strategist

888-486-4133

WhoseApple.org

The Only Thing Standing between You and Destiny is the Courage to Take the First Step

www.ingramcontent.com/pod-product-compliance
Lightning Source LLC
Chambersburg PA
CBHW060536100426
42743CB00009B/1543